Be The Best You Can Be

A Guide to Etiquette
and Self-Improvement for
Children and Teens

By

Robin Thompson

Published October 1999 by Robin Thompson Charm School
17298 Lake Knolls Road
Pekin, Illinois 61554
309.925.3157
www.etiquette-network.com

Library of Congress Card Number: 99-091463

ISBN 0-9675318-0-2

Be The Best You Can Be
Cover design by Richard IV, New York.

Printed in the United States of America

*"This book is dedicated to my parents,
Robert and Joyce Thompson,
for their love and support."*

TABLE OF CONTENTS

INTRODUCTION

BE THE BEST YOU CAN BE!

Let this be your goal throughout life. Believe it, embrace it, live it.

You are a very special person with your own personality, talents and interests. Believe in yourself to live life to the fullest. There is so much that you can offer to your family, friends and the world around you.

There is no one else exactly like you. Wouldn't the world be a boring place if everyone looked alike, dressed alike and had the same interests? It's great to have such a mix of cultures, beliefs and feelings. Meeting and getting to know others can be exciting. And it's important to know that you don't have to be like everyone else. In fact, you shouldn't want to be anyone but you.

Two of your best friends in life will be a positive attitude and a confident image. These friends will always be there when you need them. They'll help you reach your highest dreams and desires.

Learn discipline in mind and body. Use good manners and treat everyone with respect. This shows you respect yourself as well.

You're never too old to try new things, act on ideas or start a new project. Being active leaves little time for feelings of worry, doubt and loneliness.

Be in love with life and those around you. Have fun, laugh often and have a good sense of humor.

Learn from your mistakes so you can do things different the next time. But don't dwell on the blunders you've made. Humans aren't perfect. Forgive yourself just as you forgive others when they let you down.

Self-improvement is a continuing process that lasts a lifetime. Be good to yourself. You deserve to be the best you can be.

MIND YOUR MANNERS

My goal is to give you the confidence and poise that comes with the knowledge and use of good manners. Only then will you be on your way to being your best!

Let's give some definition to what manners and etiquette really mean.

Manner: a habit, behavior, a way of doing something

Good Manners: socially correct behavior, good habits

Etiquette: the rules and practices of correct and good behavior

No one gets arrested for breaking a rule of etiquette. It is not a harsh set of laws, but simple guidelines that when followed make life run smoothly.

Using good manners doesn't mean life will be dull, boring and strict. In other words, no fun. Minding your manners makes life much easier. You'll be relaxed and confident instead of nervous and insecure.

Others think they need manners only on special occasions. "Oh sure, I act nice when I go to a fancy restaurant, but why do I have to use my manners when I'm at home or just hanging out with my friends?"

Why shouldn't you? Family and friends deserve to be treated with respect and kindness too, don't they?

Don't save good manners just for special occasions. When it comes time to use them, you'll forget what to do.

Did you know that you use manners - good or bad - every time you speak, act or even think a thought?

- Have you ever been nervous and not sure of what to say or do?
- Perhaps you had trouble making an introduction?

- Were you at a friend's house for dinner and found that you hated the main course?
- Have you gotten tongue-tied around new people? Especially that certain someone you've had a crush on for months?

Manners will guide you through these times. They tell you what to do and when to do it. However, being mannerly must never make others feel inferior. Neither judge nor notice the flaws of others. Your actions should make those around you feel comfortable and at ease.

Manners aren't sold in stores. They're free to one and all. So, why aren't you using them? Perhaps you already are. Congratulations! This book will help you brush up on the basics and open your eyes to a few new ideas.

Let this thought be your guide:
Act out of consideration for others. Think about their feelings and needs before your own.

Have you ever stopped to think about someone else's feelings? Or are you so wrapped up in yourself that you forget about everyone else?

What would make the people around you happy? What would upset them? If they're happy and having fun, chances are you will too.

Do you know the golden rule?
Do unto others as you would have them do unto you.

Treat people as you would like to be treated. How do you feel when someone is unkind to you? Upset, sad, hurt? No one likes to be teased, lied to, gossiped about or picked on. Suppose someone makes a rude remark to you. Your first thought is to hurl an equally bad comment right back. That's wrong. Never lower yourself to their level. Rise above it.

You have choices in life: to be nice or rude, thoughtful or inconsiderate, positive or negative, use good manners or bad manners. Choose wisely. Your rewards will be endless.

LEARN TO LOVE YOURSELF

PROJECTING A POSITIVE IMAGE

**Who is your best friend? Chances are you've never said,
"I am!"**
**But haven't you known yourself longer than any of your other
friends? Haven't you had time to become the type of person
you would want to have as your best friend? Why should
anyone else like you if even you don't like yourself?**

Do you have an "if only" list? "If only I were prettier, if only I
were thinner, if only my parents made more money, life would be
perfect and all my problems would disappear." Do you think that
would really happen?

It's so easy to tell others how to fix their flaws. It's much harder to
improve our faults, but it can be done. Why are we so hard on
ourselves? It seems we're never happy with our looks and our
bodies. Learn to like yourself, flaws and all, but always be open to
self-improvement.

Let's talk about image. Your image is how you imagine yourself to
be. It's a picture of you in your mind. You have a self-image which
is how you see yourself, and a public image which is how everyone
else sees you.

You're in control of your self-image. You also have a lot of control
over how others see you. This depends on what you say, how you
look and how you treat them.

Your self-image may or may not be the "real" you. Usually, we
hold a lower image of ourselves than we should. We put ourselves
down, ignore our strengths and expect too much of ourselves. A
negative self-image often causes boredom, loneliness and shyness.
All the things you definitely don't need.

A positive attitude is learned—you aren't born with it. But we grow up hearing many negative messages. "Don't do this, don't do that, don't speak unless you're spoken to." In fact, the first three words a baby usually learns are "mama," "dada," and "no!" Those of you who baby-sit know the importance of saying "No," at times. But we need positive words of encouragement from our parents just as much.

Do you have any strengths hiding behind a negative attitude? Why not take a look?

Who is holding you back from becoming the best person you can be? You are. You can achieve all you want if you do something about it now.

● Take action. Start thinking about what you can do instead of what you can't do.

● See yourself as you want to be: looking great, smiling, feeling happy. Carry this mental picture in your mind all day long.

● Most people worry more about their appearance than their attitude. Looks may not last, but a positive attitude does. Attitude affects everything about you.

● Stop comparing yourself to others — "I'm not as attractive, smart, popular." Would you truly trade places with someone else? You are unique. There will never be another person exactly like you. Be proud of who you are.

● Don't guess what others are thinking; you will usually guess wrong. Just because some people are laughing when you walk by them does not mean they are laughing at you. Haven't you ever been laughing and joking with your group of friends while others walked by?

● Make a promise right now to replace all negative thoughts and worries with good, positive thoughts. Be poised! Let go of negative feelings like envy and revenge. These emotions can literally make you sick. A poised person does not waste time on such feelings.

- Say this statement aloud, "Confidence and a positive attitude will take me further than looks and money." You may not believe it, but it's true. Think about some of the people you know who are attractive but only concerned with material things and money. Are they happy, nice and caring?

- When you get up in the morning, look in the mirror and say, "Hello, _____. We will have a great day today."

- You are in control of what you think, say and do. No one pulls your strings. If you choose to be in a bad mood all day, you have only yourself to blame.

- Don't blame everyone else for your problems (mom, dad, siblings). Take responsibility for your own actions.

- Take people's remarks in stride. If anyone makes a cruel comment or insult, it usually means they're jealous or intimidated by you. If they took the time and effort to come up to you and say something – good or bad – that also means they took the time to notice you. These are very insecure people who have to insult you to make themselves feel better. Actually, I've always been amused when someone said something bad about my fashion shows or that "modeling was dumb." They were jealous!

LIKES AND DISLIKES

Use the following pages to list the things you like and dislike about yourself. Which list is longer? I hope it's the "like" list. Learn to enjoy your good qualities; these are your strengths. How many of your dislikes can you work on changing? If you can't change them, can you at least change the way you think about them?

A girl in my current course has very curly hair. She disliked it. That is until she talked with another girl in the course who has straight hair. After listening to how many hours and how much money is spent on perms, curling her hair, spritzing it, spraying it, teasing it, only to have the curl fall out in a couple of hours, my curly-haired student admitted that all she does in the morning is mist her hair, style it with her fingers and go. And it stays curly all day! Now she considers her curls a strength.

JUST FOR YOU

Take a favorite photo of yourself and tape it to your bathroom mirror. Every morning while getting ready, look at it and see how great you look. You are very important!

THINGS I LIKE ABOUT MYSELF

Include your physical strengths—appearance, hair, height, weight—as well as personality strengths—friendly, loyal, neat, good listener, etc. Ask your parents and friends what they like about you too.

Physical Strengths

Personality Strengths

THINGS I DISLIKE ABOUT MYSELF

Let's call these areas for improvement. By knowing exactly what you don't like, you can begin turning these weaknesses into strengths. If it's something you can't change, such as height, list it anyway. You can change your attitude about it.

Physical Dislikes

Personality Dislikes

Pick the one thing that you would really like to improve and write it here: *(Example: I'm getting C's in most of my classes.)*

What would you like instead? (This is goal-setting.) *(I'd like to get B's—maybe even a few A's)*

Write in detail how you can go about doing it and how long it will take. *(Study every night for 45 minutes, complete all assignments on time. Do this for one month.)*

What reward will you give yourself for reaching and keeping your goal? *(A new CD.)*

When you have reached your goal, congratulate yourself! Then begin work on the next area for improvement. Keep it up!

IMAGE QUIZ

This quiz will help you start thinking about your image and how well you like yourself. There are no right or wrong answers so be honest and do your best.

1. I am happy with the way I am.   Agree   Disagree

2. I like these five things about me:

3. I'd like to change these five things about me:

4. At home, I am in a good mood.   Agree   Disagree

5. When I'm with my friends, I put myself
    down.   Agree   Disagree

6. Even on a bad day, I can think of one good
    thing that happened.   Agree   Disagree

7. I worry about a lot of things.   Agree   Disagree

8. I don't compare myself with other people.   Agree   Disagree

9. I'm just as good and nice as everyone else.   Agree   Disagree

10. I am shy in a group.   Agree   Disagree

11. I am happy with my appearance.   Agree   Disagree

12. It seems no one else has problems or worries about things.   Agree Disagree

13. I see myself being successful in whatever I do.   Agree Disagree

14. I tend to blame others for my problems.   Agree Disagree

15. When something upsets me, I forget it and move on with my day.   Agree Disagree

16. I am not afraid to try new hobbies, activities, etc.   Agree Disagree

17. Other people have better, easier lives than I do.   Agree Disagree

18. I don't judge others by their appearance.   Agree Disagree

19. I look in the mirror front and back before heading out the door.   Agree Disagree

20. I try to be a positive person in thought, word and deed.   Agree Disagree

1. agree	2. fill in	3. fill in	4. agree	5. disagree
6. agree	7. disagree	8. agree	9. agree	10. disagree
11. agree	12. disagree	13. agree	14. disagree	15. agree
16. agree	17. disagree	18. agree	19. agree	20. agree

FIRST IMPRESSIONS

Is it right to judge someone by a first impression? No! Of course not. But as unfair as it may be, people judge you by the way you look, dress, sound and act. Nowhere are your actions and physical appearance more important than when you meet someone for the first time.

Judging others without getting to know them first isn't fair. But we've all done it. It doesn't take long either. First impressions are formed within 6 seconds! It's important to present an image that makes others want to get to know you better. Everything you do from the moment you meet the other person - shaking hands, smiling, saying hello, sitting down, conversing and keeping eye contact - really does matter.

Pay attention to what you wear. Walk with poise and good posture. Smile, look the person in the eye, speak loud enough to be heard and use good grammar. By doing this, you're silently stating, "I care about myself, and I want you to care about me too."

WHAT'S REALLY IMPORTANT?

Eyes
Maintaining eye contact shows poise and confidence. The eyes say a lot. Make them say what you want.

Handshake
Give a firm, brief handshake that's not too hard, not too wimpy. Continue shaking hands while you introduce yourself. Don't shake hands by holding just the fingertips. Don't worry about having cold hands or sweaty palms.

Laughter
Develop a soft, easy going laugh. A shrill, cackling laugh is irritating and annoying.

Voice
Many of my students used to speak too soft. If you want others to enjoy your company, speak loud enough to be heard. I can't begin to describe the bad impression that is given when you don't speak up. **A barely audible voice actually shouts to others, "I don't think enough of you to speak up. I'm shy. I don't care about my image."**

Posture
Stand and sit straight and tall. Don't slouch or fidget. Be still.

HAVE A WINNING SMILE

Beautiful hair, flawless skin, designer clothing, that's all you need, right? WRONG!

You need the one thing that is free and on call 24 hours a day. A great smile is your best feature. Smiles are easy to use and never go out of style. They make you look confident. People are drawn to smiles. A smile comes in handy when you're nervous. If you have to give a speech in class, put on a big smile and act as if you're having a great time. No one will know differently.

Do you look bad in pictures? Does your smile look fake? Look in the mirror and smile. Is your face stiff? Is your head tilted down? Do your eyes squint because you smile "up"?

For a perfect smile: Relax your jaw, don't tighten facial muscles. Keep eyes open. Smile "out" toward your cheeks. Practice saying, "Ha, ha, ha." Your smile should come easily and naturally as if you've never practiced it. But practice makes perfect, right?

WHAT KIND OF FIRST IMPRESSION DO YOU MAKE?

Would you be impressed if you could meet yourself? How do you think you'd look and act?

Practice in front of the bathroom mirror. Pretend to introduce and shake hands with yourself. Hold a mock conversation. Watch your body language. Set a mirror in front of you the next time you're on the phone. Watch your facial expressions. This shows what you look like to others.

PERFECTLY POISED

Let's talk about poise. It's a word you'll want to remember. Poise means being self-confident, balanced, in control. It means not being nervous, embarrassed and uncomfortable. Which way do you feel most of the time? You can learn how to be more poised with a bit of daily practice.

HOW TO BECOME MORE POISED

Picture yourself as you want to be. See yourself as always saying and doing the right thing. This does wonders for your self-confidence. But don't let it go to your head. No one is perfect!

Think before you speak. If what you want to say will hurt someone's feelings, don't say it. Say only words that are kind and good.

Move slowly and think about your actions. Take your time. Fast, thoughtless movements show nervousness. Slower, controlled movements reflect confidence. Let your image reflect a relaxed, confident person.

PERFECT POSTURE POINTERS

The old saying, "Clothes make the man," should read, "Posture makes the man...or woman."

Wearing the latest designer fashions won't help your appearance if you slouch, throw your shoulders forward and stand with your feet pointing in opposite directions.

Good posture can make you look wonderful, whether wearing jeans or formal dress. When you stand up straight and tall, you appear confident; you look like someone who has it made.

The key to good posture is to make it a habit. Use it all the time so that it comes naturally.

FOLLOW THESE TIPS TO DRAMATICALLY IMPROVE POSTURE:

1. Keep that chin up; head erect and held back. Tilting your head down makes your neck disappear. Don't stick your nose in the air. That makes you look stuck up.

2. Keep shoulders back, but relaxed. This automatically lifts your chest, another posture pointer.

3. Stretch long through the body; think tall. Your clothes will look better this way.

4. Tuck your behind under; this tilts the pelvis forward. Don't arch your back.

5. Do not lock your knees. Pushing your legs back throws good posture out of whack.

6. Toes should be pointed straight ahead; feet close together.

7. Arms stay close to your sides, palms in, elbows slightly bent. Fingers are relaxed, never clenched tightly or pulling on clothing.

WALKING TALL

Walking is one of those things you do everyday, but do you pay any attention to it?

You have a certain walk. People who know you well will be able to recognize you by the sound of your footsteps. Work on your walk until it feels light and controlled. A bad walk wears you out and creates a negative, lasting impression.

STEPS TO A PERFECT WALK

- Before you start, remember the tips on becoming more poised and your posture checklist.

- Begin by using your thigh to pick up your foot. Don't throw your foot forward without first lifting it up off of the floor.

- Use your knee joint to place your foot forward. The order is to first lift your leg and then place your foot forward. This prevents shuffling your feet.

- Your heel should touch the floor first—then quickly shift the weight forward to the entire foot as you take the next step. This keeps your step light.

- Keep toes pointed straight ahead.

- Never walk on the inside/outside of your shoes.

- Don't walk too fast. Be in control. Take a natural stride.

- Arms never swing wildly but glide back and forth with fingertips brushing alongside your body.

- Keep your head up and look straight ahead. You don't have to look at your feet to make them work.

- Practice in all of your shoes, not just flats or sneakers. If you buy a new pair of shoes for a special occasion, break them in by wearing them around the house at least one week before the event. You may learn a painful lesson if you wear brand new shoes to a dance where you're on your feet all evening.

Is your walk graceful, controlled? Is it eye pleasing?
Or do you stomp and plod along for all the world to hear?

Have some fun while you're practicing.

Imagine that you're a presenter at the Academy Awards. Millions of people are watching as you make your way to the podium. You know you look great because you've practiced hard, and now your good posture and confident walk come naturally. You're able to enjoy the evening without worrying about tripping and falling off the stage.

SITTING PRETTY

Take a look around at your fellow classmates. Are they sitting up straight, feet together under the desk or are they sprawled out, feet in the aisle? Maybe they're cracking knuckles, chewing on their pens, biting their nails.

Do they look impressive?

Sitting still and using good posture take concentration but are habits worth cultivating. It shows a great deal of poise and confidence.

PLEASE BE SEATED

- There are two things you should never do:
     Don't grab the chair. It won't run away from you.
     Don't lean forward at anytime. Think straight and tall.
- Practice using a sturdy chair. Don't use a soft, low couch.
- Walk over to the chair and let the back of your right leg touch the front right side of the chair. Turn your body to the right a bit. You always look better at an angle than facing straight ahead. Place your body weight on your right leg.
- Sit down without leaning forward. Use your hands to guide you as you sit on the edge of the seat, then slide back. Make sure that you are still turned to the right a bit. The exception to this is if you're at a dinner table or desk. Then you face it squarely.
- Once seated, keep feet together and under the chair.
- Women always keep their knees together.
- When sitting in a straight-backed chair, don't tip it back so that it's rocking on two legs. You could tip too far and topple over.
- Crossing your legs isn't good for them. But if you insist, remember that for women, crossed legs rest against one another. Never swing them.
- Don't sit with one foot underneath you. Never twine your legs around the chair legs.
- Pull up on your pant legs a bit when sitting so they won't ripple.
- To stand slide forward and rise to the occasion. Use your hands to scoot forward on the seat and then stand with a straight back.
- Don't stand up so fast that you push the chair out from underneath you.

Review

1. The most important part of good manners is:

2. What is the golden rule?

    How can you put it to use in your everyday life?

3. Have you seen any examples of bad manners recently?
    If so, list them:

4. Pretend that you have a new pen pal who wants you to
    describe yourself—both in appearance and personality. What
    could you write?

5. What do you like most about yourself?

6. What do you like least about yourself?

7. Do you make a good first impression? Practice in front of a mirror. Introduce and shake hands with yourself. Make small talk. Watch your facial expressions, eye contact and body language. Listen to your voice. Now try it again with Mom or Dad as a partner. Ask how you did and take their advice!

8. Define poise:

9. Describe a time when you needed to be poised but were not:

10. How can you become more poised?

11. List two people you know who have good posture:

   1.

   2.

12. The seven steps for perfect posture are:

   1.

   2.

   3.

   4.

   5.

   6.

   7.

13. List at least three things necessary for a perfect walk:

14. What two things should not be done when sitting down?

15. Where should feet be placed while sitting?

VOICE

"It doesn't matter what I sound like, my friends will still listen to me," said my student whose voice was not one of her strengths. Yes, it's true. Her friends may hear her, but they won't like what they're hearing. Voice is a big part of your image. It's one part you can easily improve.

How does your voice sound? If you haven't heard it on tape lately, get out the tape recorder. There are many ways to get the "real you" on tape. Call a friend and chat for ten minutes or record the family dinner conversation (let them know about it). Play the tape back. Does it sound like you? Probably not. But that's how you sound to others. Make notes on what you like and dislike.

Voice 101 isn't offered in school yet, so here's a crash course on how to sound great.

- **How** you say it is as important as **what** you say. If your voice is loud, shrill or annoying, few people will listen. Would you?

- Speak slowly and clearly. Everything you say will sound better. Of course, the slower you speak, the better you can pronounce words. Don't be in a rush to get your thoughts out. Speaking slowly gives you more time to think about what to say next. You'll sound smarter! What happens to your voice when you're nervous? You speak quickly. So slow down and speak up. When you give a speech in class, write "slow down" at the top of the page.

- Smile while speaking. This makes you sound confident and happy no matter how you feel inside.

- Pronounce the entire word. "Going" is not "goin'" and "picture" is not pronounced "pitcher." Opening and shutting your mouth are not the only requirements necessary for speech. Use your lips and tongue to form the words.

- Speaking softly or loudly are equally annoying and rude. Speak loud enough so others can hear you. That shows maturity. Keep a softer voice in the library, at church and similar quiet zones.

- Breathe deeply. There has to be enough air in you to project your voice.

- Choose your words carefully. Use good grammar. Cut out the slang. Don't use any words that would offend or hurt others including your family.

VOICE HELPERS

Singing
Whistling
Reading aloud
Saying the alphabet slowly in front of a mirror

Tongue twisters:
Holding the jaw still, teeth clenched together, say:
> "He thrust 3,000 thistles through the thick of his thumb."
> "The sea seaseth and it sufficeth us."

If you don't think the sound of your voice is important, answer this:

How believable would your teacher sound with Donald Duck's voice?

What if the President came on television to announce a national crisis, except his voice was replaced with that of Mickey Mouse? Would you take him seriously?

CONVERSATIONS

Communication is a lot more than tossing out some words to your listening public. It's an art that takes practice. But if you consider how much time you spend talking, shouldn't you be an expert by now? After all, it's a skill used practically every minute of each day.

Is it easy for you to meet strangers? Can you talk to them without being nervous?

If you said no, don't feel too bad. Most people have a tough time talking with new acquaintances.

You converse with parents, friends and teachers. You make small talk with store clerks, receptionists and your doctor, so you already have lots of practice.

It's a mark of good manners to know how to start a conversation. The easiest way to begin is by asking a question. In the perfect conversation the other person responds, asks you a question and on it goes.

Conversation is not one-sided. Would it be fair if you did all of the talking? Of course not. Nor is it fair if you say nothing at all.

Do you have any friends who monopolize your conversations— they do all of the talking and none of the listening? When you finally get a word in, they interrupt and start off on another story of their own.

Be a good listener. Pay attention and keep an open mind. Listening encourages others to talk more, and that helps if you can't think of anything to say. I would rather be known for the way I listen than the way I talk. You learn only while listening.

Silence during a conversation helps by giving you time to think— about what has been said and what you'll say next.

Use good grammar, always. Sloppy grammar shows laziness. Do you say *um, uh-huh, huh-uh, yeah*? How many times do you say *really, like, you know* or other repetitive words?

HOW TO TALK TO ANYBODY

- Memorize several topics you can talk about. Stick to the basics. Ask about family, school, hobbies, sports, movies, books, TV shows, vacations, pets, famous people, church. If a new student moves into town, ask where she lived before and what she liked about her town.

- Never ask personal questions. Money is not a good topic. "How much did your outfit cost?" "How much money do you make?" That's being nosy. The same is true for questions about weight. This goes for thin people as well as those who are overweight. Why does it matter how much someone weighs? Age is another no-no. Don't ask an adult's age. Again, it's none of your business.

- Any question you wouldn't want to answer should never be asked.

- Unpleasant topics at the dinner table should be avoided.

- If you are asked a question that you don't want to answer, respond, "Why do you want to know?" Or simply say, "I'm not going to answer that."

- Get your point across clearly. Wars have been launched because of poor communication, not to mention rumors, lies, etc.

MORE HELPFUL CONVERSATION TIPS

- Be informed, read the paper and good books. Have opinions on world and community events.

- Don't use big, fancy words just to impress people.

- Never correct someone's grammar in front of others. It's embarrassing for that person, and you'll come off looking snobbish.

- Don't be a know-it-all. No one knows everything. You can learn a lot through conversations, just keep those ears open.

- Get to the point. Don't go on and on and on. You don't have to go into extreme detail. Hit the highlights. Keep it fresh.

- End your sentences with periods, not question marks. Drop the tone of your voice at the end of sentences. Don't raise it.

- Answer with more than a grunt or mumble. At the very least, say "Yes," or "No."

- Don't tell people what to do. Ask them. It's amazing how willing they'll be to help if you throw in a few kind words, like "Please," and "Thank-you."

- Don't lie to impress others. It doesn't work. You lose your credibility and their trust in you.

- Never curse or use profanity. It offends most people and shows your immaturity.

- Don't interrupt a person who is speaking. Wait your turn.

- You don't always have to get the last word in. Just once let someone else have the last say.

- Pay attention to the person speaking and maintain eye contact. That's being an active listener.

- Talk about positive things. Try not to be a complainer and whiner.

- Don't gossip.

BE THE LIFE OF THE PARTY

You've been invited to a friend's party. Wonderful! But don't mistakenly think that all you need to do is put on some nice clothes and go.

Actually, accepting a party invitation is accepting the responsibility for being a gracious guest.

- Your first obligation is to **promptly** tell your friend if you will be attending. R.S.V.P is French for "repondez s'il vous plait," meaning "please reply." If this term is on the invitation, you must respond. Even if you can't attend, this needs to be known too. A correct guest count helps in knowing how much food and drink to serve, how many party favors to have, the number of tables to set and so on.

- Never arrive before the stated time. Your friend's party starts at 7:30. But you can't wait to tell the latest gossip so you arrive at 5:30. Do you think your friend is just sitting around with nothing to do? No! He/she's preparing food, setting tables, getting ready. This is not the time for a heart to heart talk.

- If the party is given to celebrate an event - birthday or graduation - bring a suitable gift. Carefully give it to your friend when you arrive.

- Make a good entrance. Wait to be invited in, wipe your feet on the doormat. If it's been raining or snowing, remove your shoes. Speak to the parents if they're present. Say something nice about their house or the party decorations. Or simply thank them for inviting you.

- Make a good impression. Smile, make eye contact, carry yourself with style. Did you check your appearance, both front and back, before leaving home? Is your hair clean and shiny? Are your clothes clean and pressed? Any missing buttons or tears? What's your body language saying?

- The most important part of any party is not the food, it's the company and conversation. So talk and have a good time. Keep the conversation upbeat.

- Do your best to make the party fun for all. Be in a great mood. Don't complain that you're bored or make comparisons with someone else's party. Go along with the group by joining in the fun. Don't expect to do only the things you like.

- If refreshments are served, don't make a mad dash to the table or overdo on first helpings. When going through a buffet line, never cough on the food. Don't pick up an individual serving of food and smell it to see if you like it. Don't stick your finger in it for a quick taste either. Refrain from sarcastically asking, "What's this?" Never begin eating while you're still going through the food line. If dip is served, don't double dip (eating half the chip and dipping it again). That's like putting your mouth right in the dip bowl.

- Use good table manners: eat quietly, don't chew with your mouth open, don't slurp and smack. Handle food and drinks carefully so that you don't spill. If you do, don't try to hide it or laugh about it. Apologize and help clean it up.

- When the party is winding down, it's time to go. Don't overextend your welcome. Thank your friend and their parents; tell them you had a wonderful time. If your friend took a lot of time, effort or money in giving the party, why not write a short thank-you note telling how much you appreciated it? I promise that your thoughtfulness will be remembered for a long time.

BE A SOCIAL SUCCESS AT SCHOOL

Mention the word, **"school,"** to any student, and you'll hear groans and moans about term papers, tests and tons of homework. Going to school means lots of hard work. It is important to your future to get good grades. But school can be a surprisingly pleasant experience if you're having fun with your friends and getting along with your teachers.

Don't look at teachers as the enemy. You can learn so much from them. They've been on the same side of the desk as you. They've experienced many of the problems and emotions you face today. They're real people with feelings. Getting along with your teachers polishes the social skills you need to deal with adults.

Students and teachers alike agree that using these skills will put you at the head of the class.

SHOW RESPECT — Be a friend, but remember the teacher is in charge.

PAY ATTENTION — Your body is in class, but your mind is daydreaming a million miles away. "Oh no, is that my name being called?" "What was the question?" You learn only while listening, never while talking. That's why you're the one taking all of those notes.

DO YOUR HOMEWORK — Teachers work hard at preparing notes for class; that's their "homework." Make sure you do likewise.

BE POSITIVE — Do you like to be around people who complain and nag? No way. It's hard in the classroom when a few students voice their dislikes about everything. It's time they grow up and accept responsibility. They're getting attention, but is it the right kind of attention?

ASK QUESTIONS	You can't learn if you don't understand the subject matter. If you're too embarrassed to say, "I don't understand," say, "I didn't get all of that written down. Would you please go over that again?"
NO CHEATING	You cheat yourself when cheating on tests. Someone usually knows what you did, and it gets back to your teacher. It's not worth it.
DON'T GOSSIP	Never gossip about your teachers or anyone else. Making up or repeating gossip about anyone really shows your insecurity and immaturity. How would you like it if your teachers stood around telling stories and lies about you?
RESPECT THE DRESS CODE	Look presentable. The day you dress like a bum may be the day yearbook photos are taken. Is that how you want to be remembered? Most businesses have dress codes too. It's part of life. Get used to it.

FRIENDS

We all want friends. That's natural. But how do you do it? How do you make new friends?

First take a good look at yourself. Are you the type of person that you would want as a friend?

Picture a girl walking at school, eyes downcast, looking defensive, never smiling or speaking. Would you walk up to her and say, "Let's be friends!" I doubt it.

Are you usually in a good mood and show it? Do you care about other people and listen to them?

"Sure I do," you say, "but nobody likes me, and I'm not popular."

Remember that many of your fellow students are indifferent; they don't know you very well so they simply ignore you. Don't wait for someone else to make the first move. Plunge right in. Be yourself and don't try too hard. Smiles are invitations to conversations. Act as if the person already knows and likes you. Introduce yourself with a cheery, "Hello, I'm _____ ."

Keep the conversation simple at first. Talk about classes, extracurricular activities, hobbies or the upcoming big game.

Give a compliment as long as it is sincere, "Your hair looks great in that style." Who doesn't like to be told they look good?

Ask questions and listen when people respond. Be honest. Lying to impress someone usually catches up with you.

FRIENDSHIP FIASCOS

Take care! Thoughtless words and actions can ruin a wonderful relationship.

Friends are not possessions. It's okay for them to have other friends besides you.

Don't be a fair-weather friend. Stick by friends through good and bad times.

Be loyal. Friends are true blue! Never gossip about them behind their backs. Don't put them down. Don't desert them when they need you. Would you want them to do that to you?

Be in a good mood. We all have bad days, but don't use this as an excuse to be moody and rude.

Be delighted for friends when good fortune comes their way. If they earn an award, the top grade in class or the starring role in the school play, share in their happiness. Don't ruin it for them.

Never be jealous of a friend's possessions, such as clothes, house or family income. Wishing you had the same things is okay, but don't wish that your friends lose their material goods. There are people who have more than you and people who have much less than you. If you go to sleep tonight in a bed in your own home with a full stomach, you're very lucky.

Listen when your friend is talking. This is one of the most common complaints I hear from my students: "My friends don't listen to me. All they want to do is talk about themselves."

If a friend hurts your feelings, whether on purpose or not, don't cause a scene. Talk to him/her privately and calmly explain why you're upset. Don't accuse. Try to work things out. If they get mad or deny it, they may be embarrassed. Tell them you still want to be friends and give them time to come around. If they don't, then maybe you should find a new friend.

SHYNESS

You're at a friend's party where you see a well-dressed girl sitting all alone. Being thoughtful, your best friend, Don, sits down next to her and tries to start a conversation. She won't talk to him except for very short responses. Her eyes are turned away; she's not smiling. Is she a snob, acting very rude or just shy?

Put yourself in this girl's place. You're invited to a party, you walk in the room and realize that you don't know many people. You feel nervous, even embarrassed. You wish you were anywhere but here. Then this cute guy comes over and starts talking to you. You don't know him, so what could you possibly say? He seems so at ease and speaks so well. He's perfect. All he's doing is making you more uncomfortable. Maybe if you ignore him, he'll go away. Then you can leave.

So now what do you think? Is she a snob, acting rude? No, she's just shy.

ARE YOU SHY?

You're not alone. At one time or another, we've all been there. The problem with being shy is that you miss out on a lot of fun. Plus you may appear rude, stuck up and conceited.

Think about the times and places that made you feel shy: being at a party with no one to talk to, telling a joke and no one laughs, standing up in class and forgetting your speech, being the new kid in school. Life isn't perfect. Jokes fall flat; people forget speeches. Most of us manage to survive.

People who aren't shy may say, "Oh, that was embarrassing," but they move on without dwelling on it. And those around them won't be critical either. They're just glad it didn't happen to them.
Give yourself room to make mistakes. You learn from them.

OVERCOMING SHYNESS

● Quiet types don't have to become party animals. Everyone, even movie and rock stars, has been shy at one time or another.

- Boost that self-image. You're as important as everyone else.

- Stop worrying about what everyone thinks of you. Low self-esteem, a poor self-image, envy, the belief that everyone is better than you; all help shyness to take root in you.

- Have a positive attitude. Don't expect the worst.

- Don't feel as if you're in the spotlight every second. People aren't watching your every move. No one is filming you as you go about your day. Thank goodness!

- Fine tune those conversation skills. Be able to talk about several topics, ask lots of questions and listen.

- Say hello to one person each day, smile and maintain eye contact.

- Give people sincere compliments. They'll love you for it.

- Think about the other person and how to make him/her feel comfortable.

JUST FOR YOU

When you go to your next party or get-together, walk in smiling with head held high and make eye contact. Relax and have the attitude that you'll have a great time.

The minute you have a bad thought — "Everyone's staring at me," "No one will like me" — stop and say, "I'm poised and in control." "I'm having a wonderful time."

Practice at home before you go. Have mom or dad play the role of a party guest. Introduce yourself and make small talk. You may think you're doing it right, but ask your parent for their opinion, and LISTEN to what they say. Their impression of you may be different than the one you think you're giving.

HOW ARE YOU DOING?

List the steps you're taking to overcome shyness. Write one step daily for a week.

1.

2.

3.

4.

5.

6.

7.

Have you noticed any positive results? If so, list them here.

Review

1. Under **Voice** you learned that _____ is as important as what you say.

2. Tape record your voice. Play it back and write down how you sound.

3. Should you smile while speaking?

    Why?

4. The easiest way to begin a conversation is:

5. A person with good manners is a good listener.

   True or False

6. You learn only while talking.

   True or False

7. Silence is not necessary in a conversation.

   True or False

8. List four topics of conversation you might use upon meeting a new classmate.

9. Avoid these two topics of conversation:

10. How would you respond to a rude or nosy question?

11. How can you make a good impression when attending a party?

12. It's OK to gossip about your friends when
    they aren't around.   True or False

13. Are you happy or jealous for friends when good fortune comes their way?

14. What qualities do you look for in friends? Circle the good features that you would like your friends to possess:

LOYAL	MOODY
STUCK UP	JEALOUS
BOY CRAZY	PROMISE BREAKER
LIAR	GOSSIP
GOOD LISTENER	HONEST
MEAN	THOUGHTFUL
DEPENDABLE	UPBEAT
LOUD	FUN
POOR SPORT	PUSHY
TRUSTWORTHY	CONFIDENT

15. How would you help a friend overcome shyness?

SOCIAL SKILLS QUIZ

This quiz is designed to help you deal with others in social settings. Please answer yes or no.

1. Can you start a conversation? _____

2. List five conversation topics:

3. Are you a loyal friend? _____

4. Do you keep your promises? _____

5. Are you a poor sport when you lose? _____

6. Do you think you fit in well at school? _____

7. When you're with friends, do you insist on doing what you want to do all of the time? _____

8. Do you think you must agree with friends when you feel that they're wrong? _____

9. Will you eat whatever food is served at your friend's home? _____

10. Do you discuss your day with your parents over dinner? _____

11. Do you ask your parents what happened during their day? _____

12. Have you read a book in the past month? _____

13. Can you talk with people without feeling nervous? _____

14. Are you good-natured and fun to be with at home with your family _____?

15. Do you ignore your teachers when you see them in public? _____

16. Do you introduce yourself to new students at school? _____

17. Do you like to gossip? _____

18. When you make friends, do you look only for popular people? _____

19. When you call a friend and a parent answers, do you say "Hello," and ask how they are? _____

20. Do you have a hobby, take lessons or belong to a club? _____

21. Are you a good listener with friends as well as family? _____

22. Do you use good grammar in your conversations? _____

MANNERS AT HOME

Using good manners at home makes life easier and more pleasant for everyone. How well you treat your family reflects on you!

Your life at home prepares you for adulthood. Home is where you learn the social skills necessary to function in society as a well rounded individual.

Parents teach not just by word but also by example. It's what we **see** that we imitate more than what we're **told** to do. A child is told not to yell; yet he sees his parents fighting with each other. Children deserve the respect and courtesy of their parents just as parents deserve the same from their children.

ANSWERING MACHINES

Why do people hate to leave messages on answering machines? Please don't hang up! Leave a message. Wait one second after the beep, then slowly and clearly say your first and last name, phone number, the time and day you called and a brief message such as, "Please call me back tonight. I have a question about class." Don't ramble.

If you're leaving a message for mom or a close friend, you don't have to be so formal. But be sure to give the reason for your call and a number where you can be reached.

Check your own answering machine often and return calls promptly.

BORROWING

The first rule of borrowing is to ask permission. The second rule is to return the item in good condition. Don't borrow things too often. Are you constantly taking your brother's favorite CDs or swiping his starter jacket without telling him? If he doesn't mind, that's great. But they are his CDs and jacket; let him have the chance to enjoy them before you wear them out. If a friend wants to borrow your favorite sweater, you don't have to agree. Simply say that you aren't allowed to lend your clothing.

ENTERTAINING YOUR FRIENDS

Get your parent's permission for your friend's visit first, but don't ask your parents with your friend standing there in front of them. Have some form of entertainment planned if possible. Maybe a couple of videos or board games. Do not whine that there's nothing to do. Do not destroy the house. Clean up all messes you make. Try to keep the noise level down, especially late at night.

If your little brother or sister keeps interrupting you, be kind but firm. It's always more fun to play with the bigger kids. Let your mom know about junior's interruptions. Maybe he/she can have a friend over at the same time.

GREETING GUESTS AT THE DOOR

Look in the peephole or out the window. Of course if it's a stranger, and you're alone, do not open the door. If you know the caller, slowly open the door, smile, say, "Hello," and invite them to come in. Take their coats and ask them to join you in the living room or wherever. If it's your parent's friends, then go and tell your parents their friends are here. No yelling!

(YOUR) FAMILY

Home sweet home. It's where you want to go when you're lonely, tired or sick. In the perfect family everyone gets along. No one is rude or mean. Wouldn't that be wonderful?

Family members have feelings just like you and can be easily hurt by cruel words and deeds. Hateful remarks wound them deeply.

Why? Because they love you more than anyone. Friends may come and go, but your mom and dad will always be your mom and dad. The same goes for your brothers and sisters. Yet, we seem to take them for granted or treat them worse than we treat friends or even total strangers. The reasoning is that you have to be nice to friends or they won't be your friends any longer.

Do you treat your family as well as you treat your friends?

Make the effort to look at your family in a new light; view them as human beings. Your mom was once your age; what do you think she was like? Do you think your dad ever worried about the things you worry about now? Why not ask them about their youth? Get to know and appreciate your entire family.

GETTING UP IN THE MORNING

Mornings are a hectic time in most families. Parents rushing off to work; kids getting off to school. There's little time for a relaxed sit down breakfast and reading the morning paper.

So start the day out right by doing the following:

- Get up when the alarm goes off or the first time your parent calls for you.

- Don't stumble about the house in a bad mood.

- Share the bathroom so everyone can get ready.

- Smile and say, "Good morning."

- You could be really nice and ask them if they slept well.

- If asked a question, please respond.

- Pick up after yourself, put the milk back in the fridge, dirty dishes in the sink, rinse out the shower, make your bed.

- Say, "Goodbye," when you leave. Why not add, "Have a great day!"?

- It never hurts to tell your parents you love them. They need to hear it often.

GIFTS

What's better than getting a gift? Giving one!

Gift Giving

Think of the person for whom the gift is intended. What are their tastes and hobbies? Don't buy what YOU would like to have. Giving a gift certificate is impersonal, so make sure to match the store with the person's interests. For example, buy a certificate from your local bookstore for an avid reader. Don't give gift certificates to the same person year after year. It shows you haven't put much thought and effort into it. Gifts should always be wrapped with the card placed inside so it doesn't get lost. Giving a present in the store bag from which it came is tacky. While your gift is being opened, just smile and be quiet. Don't say, "I didn't know what to get you, so you probably won't like it."

Gift Receiving

If you're asked what you'd like to have, please give several suitable suggestions. It's bad enough when you say you don't know what you want; it's even worse when you rattle off a long list of things. Never ask for cash. That's thoughtless.

You usually open a gift when it's presented to you. Act happy and interested. When you open it, say something nice right away even if it's not what you expected or wanted. Never cry, get upset or say something rude, "What am I going to do with this?" "I already have three of these!" After you've opened all your gifts, don't complain that you didn't get what you really wanted.

Thank the gift givers verbally, but you **must** write thank-you notes. My parents had me write the notes before I could have my presents...or cash the checks. It's amazing how quickly I wrote my thank-you notes. In the note mention the gift, "Thank you for the beautiful earrings. I'll wear them with my black dress."

Exchanging a gift is alright in some cases - a shirt is too big or you got three identical CD's. If asked by the person who gave it to you, admit that you exchanged it for another equally wonderful item.

GOING TO BED
Just because you're a night owl doesn't mean your family is. You do need a certain amount of sleep each night to be refreshed the next day. Getting at least eight hours of sleep is recommended.

If you're still up after everyone has gone to bed:
- Keep the volume low on the tv and stereo.
- Close doors quietly.
- Don't turn on hallway lights that will shine in their bedrooms.
- Speak softly.
- Don't trounce up and down the stairs.
- Walk with a light step.
- If you're coming in from being out with friends, and your parents have already gone to bed, quietly let them know you're home.

HOME WORK
No, I don't mean school work, I mean home work. If you have daily chores, do them without complaining. Offer to help without waiting to be asked. This is another sign of maturity. In this way when you need help, you're more likely to receive it. Sharing makes life easier. You'll have to give up some things at times, but you'll benefit from it too.

KEEPING PROMISES
One of the best compliments to receive is that you keep your word. Be trusted to do what you promise no matter how hard or difficult it is. If you've no intention of doing something, say so. Don't let people down.

MONEY MATTERS
Knowing how to manage money is one of the most important skills you'll ever learn. It's not how much money you have that matters, it's how you manage it.

Usually, money skills begin with the allowance you receive from your parents. Did you save some of the money each week, perhaps putting it in your piggy bank? Or did you spend it all the moment you got it?

If you need to make extra money, you'll have to work for it. Begging for an allowance advance usually works as well as asking the boss for an advance on your salary.

Next comes a part-time job. This is a good time to open a savings account. Put a little in every week.

When you earn a steady income, a checking account is helpful for paying bills. Balance it each month when you receive your statement. Remember, just because you have checks in the register doesn't mean you have money in the account.

Your family's finances should not be discussed outside the home. It's not a good conversation topic.

It makes no difference if your family is wealthy or poor; handle your money wisely. If your family has to be careful about spending money, and most families do, help out as you can. It's unfair for you to spend more than your share.

If friends want to do something that you simply can't afford, don't be embarrassed to say so. Or suggest doing something else.

Avoid buying something the moment you see it. This is called impulse buying. Wait a few days or weeks and decide if you still have to have it.

Children and teens who quickly spend their money usually grow into adults who live beyond their means. Credit cards are very appealing. But you can end up owing thousands of dollars to several credit card companies very quickly. Once in debt, it's hard to get out.

If you have more money than your friends, don't be a show off. They probably know you have more, so why tell them? Nothing is a faster turn off than a person who has to tell you about the new Mercedes she's driving, the designer dress she just bought, the three week European vacation she's taking. Good for her that she can afford to have and do all these things. But she doesn't have to brag about it. I wonder if her friends like her for the wonderful person she is or for the material things she possesses?

NEAT AND CLEAN

On a scale of 1 to 10, with 10 being perfect, how neat and organized is your room?

How neat and organized are you?

Do you put things back in their place? Do clothes get hung up, beds made, books put back in the bookcase? If you can't keep your bedroom clean, how will you care for an entire house when you're an adult?

Do you show your consideration to your family by picking up after yourself throughout the house? Are wet towels thrown in the hamper, dirty dishes put in the sink or dishwasher, shoes picked up from the middle of the family room floor?

When your friends come over, do you clean up after yourselves? Your parents and siblings are not servants. They shouldn't have to pick up after you nor should you expect them to do so.

PRIVACY

No matter how crowded a home is, each family member is entitled to some place that is his/her own. Rules should enforce this concept. Don't open a closed door, knock. Wait for permission to enter. Don't snoop in anyone's purse, closet or papers. Don't read their mail or diaries and never listen to phone conversations.

RIGHTS, RULES AND PRIVILEGES

It's good to know the definitions of these words because they don't mean the same thing. Maybe it will save you from telling your parents that because you're now sixteen you have the **right** to drive their car whenever you want. Sorry, that's a **privilege**. And it's up to your parents to grant it. Maybe if you cleaned your room and did all your chores first?

Right: Liberty due you by nature or society. You have the right to life, liberty and the pursuit of happiness according to our Declaration of Independence.

Rule:	Regulation of what you may or may not do. Cleaning your room, having a curfew, no eating in the living room are examples of rules at home.
Privilege:	Special benefit or advantage that you earn. Privileges can be lost. Come home past curfew on Friday night and lose your privilege of going to the dance Saturday night.

There are many rules to follow. Parents set the rules when you're growing up. Parents have wisdom, experience and your best interest at heart. Besides, they pay the bills. We also follow the rules of teachers and employers. Society enacts rules or laws as well. Generally the more mature you act at home, the more privileges you will receive. If you are told to do something, do it. Talk out your differences. Not getting your way doesn't mean you have to act delighted, but don't sulk, argue, slam doors or neglect your responsibilities. You may not agree with your parents, but remember they are your parents and deserve your respect. Handling rejection in a mature way will impress them.

Everyone's nice when they get their way. It's how you react when you're told "No," that counts.

FAMILY RULES

Here are some good rules for your family. Please follow them.

no name calling	be honest
no shouting	be responsible
no fighting	be in a good mood
no interrupting	be encouraging
no putting down	listen attentively
no insulting	be supportive
no lying	talk out differences
no hitting	be calm
no tantrums	be understanding
no sulking	help solve problems
no snooping	be positive

Sound impossible? Not really. Anything is possible if you really want it and work at it.

SPEECH
Don't forget your good speaking habits just because you're at home.

Good grammar is still the rule. Say "Yes," instead of "Yeah," "No," instead of "Nuh-uh."

When you're asked a question, please give a verbal response. Your mom can't hear when you shake your head. Even worse is when she asks you a question, and you totally ignore her. How rude!

Your tone of voice should be pleasant. Smile when you speak. And keep the shouting down to a minimum. If you want to talk to dad, but he's upstairs, go to him. Don't yell.

Good speech is important, but don't forget to be a good listener too. That means paying attention when someone is talking. Don't interrupt. Greet your family when you come in and tell them goodbye when you leave. You shouldn't be just a blur on your way in or out.

When was the last time you told your mom that she looked pretty or that you liked your dad's new golf shirt? Compliments are not just for friends. Parents love them. Aren't they constantly complimenting and bragging about you?

You're never too old to say, "Please," and "Thank-you."

STAIRS
Do you run up and down your stairs? Or do you ascend and descend them? You can imagine the difference, can't you? Running up and down involves stomping, bouncing and lots of noise. Ascending and descending mean gently holding the railing, turning a bit toward the railing so that you can place your entire foot on the step. You then slowly and quietly place your other foot onto the next step. It's the little things like this that make such an impression on people. They'll say, "He/She does everything with such class."

HOW NICE ARE YOU AT HOME?

Answer yes or no.

1. I stand and greet visitors when they come into my home. _____

2. I am responsible for getting up on school mornings and being ready to go on time. _____

3. I complete homework assignments on time. _____

4. I perform my chores without complaining. _____

5. I say, "Good morning," and "Good night," to family members and greet them when they come home from work and school. _____

6. I help make mealtime a pleasant experience, share my day and listen to others. _____

7. I really do my best to avoid fights and arguments. _____

8. My parents can fully trust me to be home at my curfew time. _____

9. I respect my family's privacy. _____

10. I keep my room clean and neat and pick up after myself throughout the house. _____

11. I help clean up the house before and after entertaining friends. _____

12. I give family members compliments for looking great or a job well done. _____

13. I remember special days: birthdays, anniversaries, etc. with cards and gifts. _____

14. I spend my money wisely, dividing it between fun things and necessary things. _____

15. I say, "Please," and "Thank you," at home, often. _____

16. I am aware how my actions and words affect my family's feelings. _____

17. I tell my parents that I love and appreciate them. _____

18. If I had a serious problem, I would discuss it with my parents. _____

19. I carefully take and promptly deliver phone messages. _____

20. I take responsibility for my problems and don't whine when things don't go my way. _____

All responses should be YES!

MANNERS IN PUBLIC

Using good manners in public makes life easier. Acting out consideration for other people earns their respect.

AUDIENCE MANNERS

Whether you're at the circus, the symphony, a play or listening to your friend's piano recital, remember that you are one part of the audience. If you've ever found yourself at some form of entertainment that you don't care for, make the most of it. Be patient and try to find some part that you can enjoy. Being noisy or making rude remarks about the performance ruins the enjoyment for others.

- Arrive about 15 minutes before the event starts.

- If a coat check is available, use it. Most theatre seats aren't big enough to hold you and a coat.

- The ticket-taker at the main door will take your ticket and give you back the stub. Show the stub to the first usher in the theatre, and he will seat you. Keep the stub so that if anyone claims your seats, the usher can clear up the mistake.

- Be seated by showtime. Often I've been interrupted by late arrivals climbing past me to get to their seats. It disturbs everyone if you arrive late. Most theatres with live performances will not seat you for a certain period of time once the show has begun.

- At intermission you may leave your seat. Excuse yourself as you pass those remaining seated. The house will flash the lights when intermission is almost over. Be back in your seat before the show resumes.

- Don't fidget or move your head back and forth during the performance. Think of the person behind you. Don't talk or whisper loudly. Don't chew gum or unwrap mints.

- Silence cell phones and pagers.

- Don't wear strong perfume/aftershave. It's best not to wear any fragrance in such close settings.

- Applaud at the appropriate times.

BEING AN OVERNIGHT GUEST
Blend in with the family routine. Be yourself—your best self—but don't overdo trying to make a good impression. Pick up after yourself, keep your room neat and clean. Rinse out the bathroom sink and shower after use. Make the bed. On the last day of your visit, offer to change the bedding.

BEING ON TIME
Isn't it irritating when people are late? After all, if you can be on time, why can't they? It's as easy to have the good habit of being a few minutes early as being a few minutes late. If you're frequently tardy, set your watch and clocks ahead about five minutes. When driving, don't speed to make up lost time; it only saves a minute or two. Your life is more important. If something occurs to prevent you from being on time, phone ahead and explain. On the other hand, being too early isn't good either. If you're invited for dinner at 7:00, and show up at 6:00, you may catch your hostess in her robe or in the middle of preparing the meal.

CARRYING PACKAGES
When carrying a large amount of books or bundles, use a tote bag. No one looks good struggling with packages.

COMPLIMENTS
Compliments are like gifts. And we all love to receive gifts. One of the nicest things you can do is give a daily compliment. Keep them sincere, short and simple: "Your dress is very pretty." It's best not to ask where an item was purchased in case you embarrass the person. When you receive a compliment, smile and say, "Thank you." Don't put yourself down.

DOGS

Seeing/hearing dogs accompany their owners everywhere. These are working dogs, so don't pet them unless the owner agrees.

DOORMATS

Wipe your feet each time you enter anyone's home, including your own. Remove shoes if it has been raining or snowing.

DOORS

Open the door for any man or woman needing assistance: the elderly, a person carrying packages, the handicapped—but ask first. And hold the door for the person behind you. Push revolving doors gently. Close doors quietly. When visiting a friend, ring their doorbell—once is enough. Wait. If no one comes to the door, try once more or leave. Don't go looking in windows unless you're concerned for their safety. You may leave a note that you called.

ELDERLY

Are entitled to our respect and assistance. Do little niceties—open doors, carry packages. Being elderly does not mean being senile. All those years add up to lots of wisdom. They were your age at one time, you know. You may actually learn something if you talk with them. Visit nursing homes and those who live alone, or have them into your home. You don't have to have a fancy dinner, sometimes the simpler the better.

FLAG

Whether it is in a parade or displayed during the singing of the National Anthem, honor it with respect. Stand at attention, placing your hand over your heart. Sing the anthem. The flag is not a plaything.

GETTING ATTENTION

Show-offs certainly do get people to notice them, but for the wrong reasons. Get attention for good work and being pleasant and nice.

HAND TOWELS
My friend has had the same hand towels in her bathroom for 10 years. They haven't worn out because no one wants to dry their hands on such pretty little towels. Hand towels are there for a purpose - to dry hands. Use them and leave unfolded after use.

HOSPITAL VISITS
While visiting ill friends in the hospital, don't overstay your welcome depending on how quickly your friend tires. Too many people at one time is not a good idea either. Remember that if they're really sick, they need rest, not a party. That can come later. Don't say how bad they look or tell them about someone you know who had the same thing and how horrible it was. You may touch a sick friend—they need it.

HUMOR & LAUGHTER
Some people have a great sense of humor, others do not. It all depends on how you see things. Life's a lot easier when you pack a bit of fun into it. But practical jokes that hurt or embarrass are not funny. A good laugh is great but not when it is at another's expense. Don't laugh at other's bad luck. If someone takes a fall, people immediately start to laugh. Check to see if they're all right first. Laughter can really hurt someone's feelings. However, a good sense of humor is important; what's a slumber party without the giggles?

INTRODUCTIONS
Introductions are easy when you remember a few rules. After all, you're only repeating the names of two people whom you already know. When are introductions made? Passing a friend at the mall while you're with another friend doesn't require one. But if that friend stops and talks with the two of you, then you need to introduce them.

There are three general rules as to whose name is said first:
The older person. "Grandmother, may I present my friend, Morgan Deneen."
A woman. "Aunt Betty, may I present my teacher, Mr. Smith."
A higher-positioned, (or titled) person. "Dr. Thomas, may I

present my friend, Tom." (Examples are doctors, members of the clergy, politicians, etc.)

As you can see women, the elderly and dignitaries are given the courtesy of having others presented to them. For the most part a woman's name is said first no matter to whom she's introduced.

Briefly describe how you know this person. Is he your neighbor, dentist or classmate? Do they share things in common? "Sue, did you know that Sarah plays ball at her school, too?"

To make the introduction say something similar to:
"Mom, may I present my friend, Mary Smith." "Mary, this is my mother, Joyce Thompson."
Or, "My mother, Joyce Thompson, may I present my friend Mary Smith."
Make sure to say the last name as well as the first name.
Ask your parents if your friends should call them by their first or last names. Call your friend's parents by their last name unless they tell you differently.

When you have been introduced, say, "Hello." Smile, maintain eye contact and shake hands. Repeat the person's name immediately to help you remember it.

MOVIES
People attend movies to enjoy the show. This can be spoiled by selfish people talking aloud, arriving late, kicking the seat in front of them, chewing food loudly, shaking the ice in their drinks and even talking on their cell phones! Tell the usher if you have any of these problems.

NAMES
Don't shorten or change a name unless told to do so. If someone introduces himself as Michael, don't call him Mike and vice versa. As for nicknames, check first to see if the person wants to be called by it.

TEASING

Never tease anyone, especially to the point of tears. This is extremely cruel. If a classmate is being taunted and picked on, defend him or tell the teachers. Never let it continue.

THANK-YOU NOTES

Also called **bread and butter notes**. You should write a note for gifts, especially those mailed to you, after staying at a friends overnight or for a special favor done for you by someone. Notes must be handwritten. It can be fairly short; three or four lines is fine.

TRAVELING TIPS

Vacations can be fun, but they can be ruined by your own thoughtlessness or that of others

Carry a list of important numbers and information you may need in case of an emergency: your travel agent's name and number, hotel address and number, the airline you'll be using and all flight numbers, arrival and departure times. Pack one in your suitcase and one in your billfold. Leave a copy of this list with someone at home.

Before leaving for the airport, call and confirm that your flight is on time. Flights are often delayed or even cancelled.

Treat hotel rooms as your own or better. Don't carelessly spill on the carpets, blankets or furniture. Don't shine shoes on the hotel towels. A shoeshine cloth is usually provided. Stealing items such as towels, sheets, pictures and other furnishings is illegal, and you may be charged for them.

Be quiet in the hallways and keep the TV/radio low late at night.

Don't leave valuables in your room. Safety deposit boxes are available at the front desk.

Always keep your room key with you. Don't announce your room number to anyone.

Don't allow anyone to enter your room, such as a maintenance

worker, until confirming it with the front desk. Use caution.
In better hotels a bellhop takes your key and baggage and shows
you to your room. He opens the door, carries in luggage, turns on
lights, and asks if you need anything. Tip him accordingly.

Always tell a taxi driver the address of the place you wish to go.
Don't just say, "Take me to the Empire State building." Some
unethical drivers charge tourists more by driving the longer route.
If you say the address, you sound more like a native.

Don't announce to seemingly nice strangers that you're a tourist.

Don't give out such information as your hotel, tour itinerary, etc. to
anyone you don't know. You don't have to be rude, just discreet.

Be aware of your surroundings at all times. Carry your purse so
that it can't be easily snatched.

Don't set your camera down on a table in public. If it has a strap,
wear it around your neck or wrist. If not, keep it in your purse.

While placing phone calls with a calling card, make sure that no
one sees your PIN number. The same advice holds true while
making transactions at ATM machines. If someone is lurking close
by, don't place the call or make the transaction.

If you are to meet your group at a certain time for an event, don't
be late. Especially make sure to arrive a few minutes early for
such activities as sightseeing tours, theatre performances and any
function that has a set starting time. They won't wait for
latecomers.

WHISPERING
It's considered bad manners to whisper in front of others. Why?
Because they'll think you're talking about them even if you are
not. Do whisper in church, at the movies and theatre, the library
and so forth.

POLITE TALK

You'll go far if you include a few polite phrases in your vocabulary.

I beg your pardon. Say this when you need to have something repeated. Don't say, "Huh," "What," "Come again," "I'm sorry."

I'm sorry is said as an apology or to offer sympathy. Don't say, "I'm sorry," when you need to have a sentence repeated. The correct phrase for that is, "I beg your pardon."

Excuse me. When you accidentally bump someone, interrupt them or any other little annoyance, say, "Excuse me."

Greetings. Speak to your teachers, neighbors, or parent's friends when you see them in public. Don't ignore them. They'll notice it.

Goodbyes. Hug, kiss, shake hands, wave, say goodbye — do something.

Please and thank-you. These are two phrases that need to be said often. Make it a habit. "Please," means you're considerate. "Thank you," means you're appreciative. Use these words at home, as well as in public and on the phone. If you don't use them at home, you won't use them at all.

WANTED: PUBLIC ENEMY #1

No one likes rude people, especially those in public.

Keep your temper when someone does something annoying. Don't turn little problems into bigger ones. Never lower yourself to their level.

While walking in public areas: sidewalks, going into restaurants, malls, etc., be aware of other people. If you stop to talk, don't stand in front of a door or the middle of the aisle. Walk on the right side of aisles and stairs. Pay attention to where you're going. If you do run into someone, excuse yourself immediately.

Don't impale anyone with your umbrella. Hold it close to you.

Thank people for niceties, holding a door or letting you go first in line. Do the same for others. Hold the door for the person behind you.

Watch the noise level. Talk softly in hotels, theatres, hospitals and restaurants. Please don't gossip or say something you don't want strangers to overhear.

As soon as you step off the escalator, make way for the people behind you. It's dangerous to block the exit ramp while deciding which way to go.

Have patience while waiting for any elevator. Pushing the button fifty times will not make it hurry. Step back before getting on to make room for the people exiting. When getting off the elevator, those in front go first. It would be silly for a man in front to try to stand aside to let out the women behind him.

Take it easy when using revolving doors. It's not a merry-go-round, so don't spin the door so fast that others can't enter. A man goes ahead of a woman and pushes the door for her. Only one person per slot.

At the grocery store, don't run your cart into the person ahead of you. If you need to pass someone, simply say, "Excuse me." The aisles are not raceways, so go slowly. You don't want to be the one to knock over ninety jars of Miracle Whip. Don't eat the produce while in the store. Don't block the aisle with your cart; keep it to one side so others can pass you.

Don't cut in line anywhere.

Throwing a fit and yelling at your parents both in public and at home is inexcusable. Of course, they should not yell at you either. Respect and listen to each other.

Don't litter. By now this should be old news. But everyday you can see that people still think the ground is a garbage can.

Pick up and empty your food tray at fast food restaurants; don't leave it setting on the table. The same goes at the movies; pitch your drink and food containers on the way out.

HOW NICE ARE YOU IN PUBLIC?

1. I shake hands while being introduced
   to someone.   Agree   Disagree

2. I don't use good manners at school
   because no one else does.   Agree   Disagree

3. I don't cut in line ahead of others or have
   friends save a space in line for me.   Agree   Disagree

4. I say, "Excuse me," after accidentally
   bumping into a person.   Agree   Disagree

5. When I'm a guest at a friend's home,
   I help out as needed.   Agree   Disagree

6. I write thank-you notes for
   gifts received.   Agree   Disagree

7. I cover my mouth and turn away
   when sneezing or coughing.   Agree   Disagree

8. I wouldn't invite the least popular
   class members to my party
   because I don't like them.   Agree   Disagree

9. I am kind to animals and would
   never mistreat them.   Agree   Disagree

10. It's all right to be loud and noisy
    with friends in public places—
    the mall, restaurants, etc.   Agree   Disagree

11. I interrupt others while they
    are speaking.   Agree   Disagree

12. At my friend's home, I track in mud,
    put my feet up on the furniture
    and leave dirty dishes.   Agree   Disagree

13. The car radio always has to be
    tuned to my favorite station.   Agree   Disagree

14. I don't let someone with one or
    two items go ahead of me at the
    grocery store checkout line.   Agree   Disagree

15. When riding in a car, I don't
    distract the driver by yelling,
    arguing, roughhousing.   Agree   Disagree

16. I'm protective of my brothers and
    sisters in public and at school.   Agree   Disagree

---

1. agree	2. disagree	3. agree	4. agree
5. agree	6. agree	7. agree	8. disagree
9. agree	10. disagree	11. disagree	12. disagree
13. disagree	14. disagree	15. agree	16. agree

Review

1. Do you treat your family as well as you treat your friends?

2. On a scale of 1 to 10, how neat and clean is your room?

   very messy 1 2 3 4 5 6 7 8 9 10 very neat

3. Practice greeting a guest at the door. Pretend it's a friend of the family. Have Mom or Dad be the "friend."

   Do the following:

   _____ Smile

   _____ Say hello

   _____ Invite the friend inside

   _____ Offer to take their coat

   _____ Ask them to be seated in the living room (or wherever).

   _____ Then quietly go tell your parents that their friend is here. (Don't yell.)

4. I do my daily chores without complaining.   True or False

5. I always keep my promises.   True or False

6. Read the **Family Rules** on page 50. Have all family members sign below that they will abide by these rules.

7. When you're a guest overnight, do you pick up after yourself?

8. Are you on time for appointments and social events?

   If not, how late are you?

   Why?

9. Do you give a compliment every day?

10. What do you say when you receive a compliment?

11. What should you do when the flag passes by in a parade or is displayed during the singing of the National Anthem?

12. While making an introduction, whose name should be said first?

    1.

    2.

    3.

13. How would you introduce your mom and your best friend to each other?

14. You've received a beautiful sweater as a birthday gift from dear Aunt Bea. Write a thank-you note expressing your gratitude.

15. What would you do if a group of people were teasing someone at school?

16. When you don't hear what someone says, what do you say?

17. To offer sympathy or an apology, say:

18. When you bump into someone or interrupt them, say:

19. **Please** means:

20. **Thank-you** means:

ON THE PHONE

Thank goodness for telephones. How would we survive without them?

How do you sound on the phone? Intelligent, mature, impressive?

On the phone your voice alone represents you. We can't see what you're wearing or how great you look. All we can hear is a voice.

Is it pleasant and polite? Does it match your image? It's true that an irritating voice in person is ten times worse when heard over the phone.

Whether you're calling that special person for a date or your best friend for a nightly chat, you'll want to think about how you sound. If someone is hearing your voice for the first time, make it a grand first impression.

PLACING A CALL

- Before dialing, imagine the person you're calling is seated right next to you.
- Hold the phone receiver about one inch away from your mouth. You'll be understandable.
- Let the phone ring at least eight times. Your friend may be outside or in the shower.
- If you reach an answering machine, don't hang up. After the beep, slowly say your name and number and leave a brief message.
- If you are phoning a friend and their parent answers, say, "Hello," and then ask if your friend is at home. Don't pretend the parent doesn't exist.
- Always identify yourself to the person answering, and then again to the person with whom you want to speak. Never say, "Guess who this is?"

- If you dial a wrong number, don't hang up. Excuse yourself first and then state the number you're trying to reach to see if you misdialed. Perhaps you looked up the wrong number in the phone book.

ANSWERING A CALL

- Let the phone ring twice before picking it up. The safest way to answer is simply say, "Hello."
- If you answer the phone but the caller still asks for you, reply, "This is (your name) speaking."
  Never say, "This is me," or, "This is he/she."
  Say your name.
- If the caller asks for another person, say, "Just a moment, please."
  Then quietly set down the phone and go get that person.
  Never yell for him/her.
- To find out who it is, never demand, "Who is this?"
  Say, "May I ask who is calling, please?"
- Be quiet when others are on the phone. Don't listen in on a phone conversation.
- If the person called for is not at home, say, "She's unable to come to the phone, may I take a message, please?"
- Use pen and paper to write the message, repeating the caller's name and number.
- Deliver phone messages promptly.
- If a wrong number calls, don't give your name or number. Ask the number they are trying to reach.

ON THE PHONE

DURING A PHONE CALL

- Pay attention and act interested. Keep the conversation going by asking questions.
- Do not eat, chew gum or chomp on ice.
- Keep objects out of your mouth.... hands, pencils and jewelry.
- Don't watch TV or have it turned up so loud you can't hear.
- Pronounce words clearly. Each word has a beginning and an ending. One letter or number mispronounced can be costly in time or money. "Fifteen" sounds like "fifty." "B" sounds like "D" or "V."
- Smile! You can "hear" a smile over the phone. Try it.
- There's no room for slang, poor grammar and profanity.

A FEW EXTRAS

- Don't make prank calls, even to friends. Besides being illegal, you can easily upset someone. You may be calling a person who's very ill or recently had a family tragedy.
- Never call too early in the morning or late in the evening. Just because you stay up until 1 a.m. doesn't mean everybody else does.
- Don't use someone's phone without their permission. Use a calling card or pay them for long distance calls.
- Keep parents' work numbers and a friend/relative's number by the phone in case of emergency.

Review

Making a call:

1. What do you say upon reaching an answering machine?

2. Do you always identify yourself to the person answering the phone?

3. If you reach a wrong number, don't:

   What should you do?

4. Let the phone ring _____ times before hanging up.

5. You can "hear" a smile over the phone.

   True or False

Review

Answering the phone:

1. Let the phone ring _____ times before answering it.

2. If you answer the phone, but the caller doesn't recognize your voice and asks to speak to you, reply:

3. When a wrong number calls, you should give your name and number so they don't call back.   True or False

4. Do you have your parents' work number by the phone in case of emergency?

5. The phone rings and you answer. It's an important call for your dad, but he's at work. What should you do?

6. You're home alone and the phone rings. You answer and the caller wants to speak with your mom. What should you do?

RULES OF THE RESTAURANT

- When making a reservation, give your last and first name, phone number, the number in your party, arrival time, special request (birthday), and smoking preference. Always cancel if necessary.

- Upon entering the restaurant, tell the host your name. If you check coats, you'll be given a ticket with which to retrieve them later.

- Follow the host to the table. He may assist you with your chair. Sit so that you can place one hand's width between you and the table. Keep your purse on your lap or close to your feet. Don't set it on the table or hang it from the back of your chair.

- If you are someone's dinner guest, don't be extravagant and order the most expensive entrée on the menu. Casually ask what they are having. You'll know what price range to stay in. Don't take advantage of their generosity.

- Today, most women order for themselves. Look at the waiter and speak !oud enough to be heard. If you want a food prepared in a special way, request it when ordering. Never be afraid to ask the waiter about menu items or how to eat a certain food.

- The time to tell the waiter your group will be having separate checks is when ordering. (Some restaurants don't separate checks.)

- You may see these terms on the menu:

  à la carte: According to the card. Each food item is priced and must be ordered separately.

  Table d'hôte: Table of the host. A complete meal is offered at a set price, usually a better buy.

- Act mature. If you want to be treated as an adult and shown respect, act accordingly.

- Keep voices subdued; no one at other tables cares about your conversation.

- Turn off your cell phone or at least turn down the ringer volume. If you receive a call, talk quietly or go to the lobby to complete the call.

- Use good table manners. Keep your arms close to your sides while being served and eating. Pass dishes to the right. Don't bite down on your fork—only lips touch the utensil. If you find a foreign object in your food, don't ruin everyone else's meal. Quietly tell the waiter you need a new serving. Your bill should be adjusted accordingly.

- If you can't finish your meal, tell the waiter, "I'd like to take this with me." Or you can ask for the proverbial doggy bag.

- Treat the restaurant staff with respect; they are working to serve you.

- Tip 15 percent for good service, 20 percent if it was excellent. Tip the coat check $1 for two coats. If you had very poor service, tell the host or manager and be exact about what was wrong.

- Taking a book of matches from the restaurant as a souvenir is fine. Taking a glass, utensil, plate or napkin is stealing.

- Stop in the restroom to freshen up: comb your hair, make sure no parsley is hiding in your teeth, wash hands.

YOU MEAN I ORDERED THAT?

Foreign words on a restaurant menu need not be intimidating. Instead of pointing to an item on the menu, ask the waiter for the pronunciation and meaning.

agneau (ah nyoh´) lamb

ail (ah´ yuh) garlic

antipasto (an´ tih pas´ toh) Italian appetizer of fish, smoked meats, vegetables

au gratin (oh grah´ tin) topped with bread crumbs and cheese

au jus (oh zhoo´) with meat juice/gravy

au vin blanc (oh vahn blonk) with white wine

au vin rouge (oh vahn roozh´) with red wine

beurre (bùhr) butter

beurre noir (boer nwa´) browned butter

bifteck (beef´ tehk) steak

bisque (bisk) cream soup of fish or vegetables

blintz (blints) thin pancake rolled and filled

bœuf (buhf) beef

bombe (bohm´ buh) shaped frozen dessert

borsch (borsht) Russian beet soup

bouillabaisse (boo yuh behz´) Mediterranean fish stew

bouillon (boo´ yon) clear broth

brie (bree) semi-soft cheese

en brochette (en bro shet´) food on a skewer

cafe (kah fay´) coffee

cafe au lait (kah fay´ oh leh´) coffee with milk

cafe creme (kah fay´ krehm) coffee with cream

canard (ka nar´) duck

champignons (shan pen yon´) mushrooms

chad (shoh) hot

chocolat (shah ko lah´) chocolate

coq au vin (kok´ oh vahn´) chicken in wine

Coquillage (koh kee yahzh´) shellfish

creme (krem) cream

crêpes (krehp) delicate pancakes

crevette (kruh veht´) shrimp

croissant (krwa san´) crescent shaped pastry

croquette (kro ket´) minced food, shaped, coated and deep
fried

demitasse (dem´ ee tas´) small cup of black coffee

en croute (ahn kroot´) baked in a crust

escargot (es car go´) snails

filet mignon (fi lay´ meen yon´) boneless beef tenderloin;
mignon means darling, favorite

florentine (flor´ en teen) with spinach

foie (fwah) liver

foie gras (fwah grah´) pâté made with duck liver

fraise (frehz) strawberry

froid (frwah) cold

fromage (fro mazh´) cheese

fruits de mer (frwee duh mehr) seafood

gâteau (ga toe´) cake

glace (glahss) ice; ice cream

haricots verts (ah ree´ ko vehr´) green beans

homard ('o mar´) lobster

hors d'oeuvre (or durv´) appetizer

jardiniere (zhar´ de nyar´) garnished with vegetables

leau (loh) water

noix (nwah) nuts

nouilles (new wee´) noodles

œuf (oef) egg

oignon (on nyohn´) onion

pâté (pa tay´) spread or moulded ground meat

petits fours (pet´ ee forz´) small decoratively iced cakes

poisson (pwah shoh´) fish

pomme (pohm) apple

pomme de terre (pohm´ duh tair´) potato

porc (pohr) pork

potage (po tazh´) soup

poulet (poo lay´) chicken

prosciutto (pro shoo´ toh) Italian cured ham, sliced thinly

ragoût (rah goo´) stew

riz (ree) rice

the (tay) tea

tournedoes (tor ne doe´) slices of beef filet

EATING MADE EASY

TABLE MANNERS

How many meals do you eat every year? If you're like the rest of us, you have three meals per day. Multiply that by 365 days, and you come up with a grand total of 1,095 times to practice good table manners.

Use these tips daily at home so they become good habits. You'll feel much more comfortable when dining at nice restaurants. However, there may be times when you don't know what to do. That's okay. Relax and casually look around to see what others are doing. You'll learn a great deal by observing, or simply ask the waiter what to do. "You know, I've never had caviar before. What's the best way to eat it?"

Arrival for a meal
Be on time. Don't make your family wait on you. If you're invited to a dinner, never make the hostess and other guests wait. Dining is more fun when everyone's in a good mood. Eat what's being served. No negative comments about the food. "This again?" "I hate spinach!"

Burps
It's not amusing to draw attention to burping. Burp quietly and cover your mouth. Say, "Excuse me."

Blowing your nose
Eating hot soups or spicy foods can make your nose run. Dabbing at your nose with a tissue is fine. But if you have a cold and need to blow your nose, excuse yourself and journey to the restroom. Always wash your hands with soap. Napkins, especially cloth napkins, are never used as a tissue. Ick!

Beverages
Drinks are made for sipping quietly, not guzzling. Pay attention when reaching for your glass so that you don't knock it over. Hold the glass with all fingers clasped around it - unless it's a white wine or champagne glass which is held by the stem. Don't crook your pinky. Swallow your food before you take a drink.

Buttering rolls

Bread and rolls are finger foods. Tear off a bite-sized piece and apply butter using your butter knife. Butter and then eat only one piece at a time. Try not to get crumbs on the table. Place rolls on the bread and butter plate. If one is not present, place rolls on your dinner plate. However, if a basket of bread is served at the start of the meal before you have any plates, this means the bread is placed directly on the table. A waiter will 'crumb' the table to tidy up. At most American restaurants, rolls are served with the main course and are placed on the dinner plate.

Conversations

The most enjoyable part of any meal is the conversation with your dinner companions. Don't bury your head in your plate and eat as fast as you can. Talk with each person on either side of you. Choose upbeat, happy topics, nothing gross or disgusting. Eat small bites of food so you can answer a question if asked. After the meal is over, you should have memories of a good conversation, not just what you ate for dinner.

Coughing

Always cover your mouth and turn away from food and guests. If a coughing attack is coming on, excuse yourself and go to the restroom. Wash your hands.

Cutting food

Cut no more than several pieces of food at a time. Don't cut it up all at once. It's much easier to place a large piece of meat in a doggy bag rather than lots of tiny, little pieces. If you're right handed, hold the fork in left hand with prongs down and knife in right hand. Cut in one direction, don't saw back and forth. You may eat the food without switching the fork back to your right hand. Or you may switch. Either is acceptable.

Dietary Restrictions

Some people are restricted from eating certain foods due to religious beliefs and health limitations including allergies. If you're having guests for dinner, it's thoughtful to ask if they have special dietary needs. If you are invited to dinner, you may tell the hostess about your diet. But don't be too demanding or take advantage of the situation. You may decline servings of those foods which you cannot eat.

Dirty dish
If you're at someone's home, quietly ask the hostess for another dish/plate. At home, throw out cracked and broken dishes.

Eating
The key to eating is remembering the rule of good manners: act out of consideration for others - in this case your dining companions.

There will be enough food for all, so don't take huge helpings. Later on you may ask for seconds. Don't say no to any first serving even if it's a food you dislike. This is the way you learn to like new foods. Don't be a picky eater. It's fine to say, "No, thank-you," to a second serving of the dreaded liver. The exception to the first serving rule is if you are on a restricted diet or are allergic to that particular food.

Wait until everyone has been served before you begin eating. If you're at a friend's house or dining out, wait for the hostess to begin. Take your time and eat slowly. Lift your fork to your mouth. Don't curl your body over so that you appear to be a "C." Chewing with your mouth open is taboo. So is taking extremely large bites of food. Of course, you know not to talk with your mouth full. Fingers are not a finger food; don't lick them. And don't use them instead of your utensils. Don't scrape the plate with your knife.

Eat quietly: no smacking, slurping, chomping or other equally disgusting sounds.

Fingerbowls
Presentation of a fingerbowl is a nice touch. It's a small bowl filled with water and is used to cleanse your fingers. Usually, it is presented after the main course. Gently dip just the fingertips in the water and dry them with the accompanying towel keeping hands lower than the table. If no towel is presented, use your napkin. Sometimes a fingerbowl is served with the dessert plate underneath it. Don't let this confuse you. Lift the fingerbowl off the dessert plate and set it above the plate. Use the fingerbowl after dessert.

Finger foods
Sandwiches, crackers, chips, breads and rolls, cookies - break in
half if very large, carrot and celery sticks, radishes,
chicken - if at home, on a picnic or if your hostess says okay,
crisp bacon, barbecued spareribs, grapes, candy - if it's boxed
candy, pick up the candy with the little paper (called a frill),
cheese cubes, olives and artichoke leaves.

Flatware
Other names are utensils or silverware. Very simply, it means forks,
knives and spoons. Hold them properly. Don't grasp them as if
you're shoveling. Start with the outer utensil first - the one farthest
from the plate. Once it has been used, don't set the utensil back on
the table. It stays on the plate. Eat the food on your fork or spoon
in one bite, not several small bites. Only your lips touch the fork,
not your teeth. Don't bite down on the forks tines scraping them
through your teeth. That noise is irritating to many just like
fingernails on a blackboard.

Food lodged in teeth
It's a good idea to take a quick look in the restroom mirror to check
teeth and lips for "leftovers" before leaving a restaurant. Picking at
the piece of spinach lodged between your teeth while at the dinner
table is a no-no. Go to the restroom and use dental floss or even a
toothpick to remove any food particles. Be sure to rinse the sink.

Foreign object in food
The main rule here is don't cause a scene. Let's say you're dining
with your friend's family, and you find a hair in your food. Just
push it aside. It wasn't put there on purpose, and it certainly won't
kill you. So save your friend from embarrassment and let it go. If
it's something worse, maybe a bug, ask for another serving. A
savvy hostess won't ask why. If she does, quietly tell or you can
leave that particular food uneaten. Being at a restaurant is another
matter. Discreetly call the waiter and say that you need another
serving.

Fork foods
When in doubt whether to eat a certain food with your fingers or a fork, use the fork. The less you use your fingers the better. Some fork foods are: pastries with filling, eggrolls, deep dish pizza, deviled eggs, chicken - if served in a restaurant or friend's house, watermelon, french fries - you can use your fingers at fast food restaurants, asparagus, cupcakes, bananas - when eaten in a restaurant, most seafood such as shrimp, clams and lobster, shish kebabs - hold the skewer with one hand and use the fork to slide the meat and vegetables onto your plate (since skewers are metal and may retain heat, be careful not to burn yourself).

Grace
Prayers are offered before the meal. Don't take food or perform any other action that would interfere with this serious moment.

Hot food
Always take a small first bite of food or sip of beverage to check the temperature. You won't burn your mouth this way. If it's too hot, wait until it cools a bit. Don't stir up the food or spread it around on your plate to cool it. That's for kids.

Leaving the table
Some parents tell their children to ask for permission to be excused from the table. That's fine, but it's inconsiderate of parents to expect their children to sit quietly for half an hour after the meal is over while the parents chat about this and that. If you need to use the restroom while at a restaurant, say, "I need to freshen up."

Napkin
A napkin is placed across your lap after grace is said. Use a napkin to pat, not wipe, your mouth as needed and before drinking your beverage. Also use it to clean your hands. It remains on your lap the rest of the time. There is no excuse for licking your fingers. A napkin is not a tissue, never use it to blow your nose. After the meal, place your napkin on the left side of the plate. Don't refold it. Ladies wearing lipstick should be careful not to leave a "lipstick kiss" on a white cloth napkin. Use a tissue to blot your lips before dining.

Passing food

Pass to the right. After helping yourself to a serving of food, don't leave the dish next to you. Pass it around the table to make sure everyone has been served. Then you may begin eating. Be careful passing hot dishes. Make sure there's a place to set it down before you pick it up. Pass pitchers and serving dishes with the handles turned toward the receiving person. If you pass your plate to receive another serving, line up the knife and fork on the right side of the plate. Salt and pepper should be passed together. It's easier to keep track of them.

Please and Thank-you

Say these thoughtful words often. Say, "Please," when asking for something, "Thank-you," when receiving it and "Yes, please," or "No, thank-you," when offered another serving. Thank your hostess for a wonderful afternoon or evening, not just for the meal itself.

Posture

You can probably figure out what I'm going to say. Don't slouch or lean forward while eating. Sit straight and close to the table. The old rule is that you should be able to place the width of your hand between the table and your body. Traditionally, elbows stay off the table during the meal. While raising your fork to your mouth, elbows stay close to the body keeping them pointed downward. Legs and feet stay under the chair. Keep feet on the floor, don't swing them. Don't kick or tilt your chair. Sit still, be poised. No playing footsies with the person seated across from you.

Removing food from mouth

A simple rule - be discreet. Use your fingers to remove cherry pits and grape seeds; use a fork to remove a piece of gristly meat. If you put the food in your mouth with your fingers, use your fingers to remove it; the same with your fork. After removing the food from your mouth, set it on your plate. Don't hide it in your napkin or underneath the plate.

Seasoning food

Wait until you've tasted your food before adding seasonings. Be careful not to insult your host and hostess. They may have spent a great deal of time marinating the filet or preparing a delicious bernaise sauce for the entreé. How will they feel when you ask for the ketchup?

Serving
There are many ways to serve food. Plates may be prepared in the kitchen and brought to you or the host may fill the plates at the head of the table. If food is brought to the table, it should be placed in bowls or serving dishes. Leave the pots and pans in the kitchen. Milk cartons, cottage cheese containers, bread in plastic bags don't belong on the table. There will be times when you'll be in a hurry or eating alone and won't be so proper. You can bend the rules once in a while.

In restaurants, servers should present your food from your left if possible and remove dirty plates from the right. Dishes are not stacked as they are removed either at home or in public. The table should be cleared of all used plates and bowls before dessert is served. It's unappetizing to be served a new course, dessert, when the remains of the last course are still on the table. Why is it that the turkey that looked so delicious before dinner loses its appeal when the chocolate mousse arrives?

Sharing
If you want a taste of food from someone else's plate, first ask if you may try it. Pass them your fork so they may give you a bite or allow them to pass their plate to you so you can take the item off it. Utensils are not shared. One bite is all you should ask for. Eating all of your neighbor's french fries isn't nice. And don't keep asking, "Are you going to finish that?" With restaurants serving such large portions, many people choose to share a meal. That's fine, but ask for two plates.

Smoking
If a group is going to dinner, the smokers yield to the non-smokers and sit in the non-smoking section. A smoker can always get up and go out for a cigarette. In the home no one should smoke while you're eating.

Soup
Placing your soup spoon in the soup, dip the spoon away from you, not toward you. Lean in a bit as you raise the spoon to your mouth. This prevents spills. Sip from the side of the bowl of the spoon, don't put it all the way in your mouth. Eat quietly, no slurping. You may eat crackers along with your soup. You aren't supposed to

crumble them directly in your soup. This is another rule that may be bent. Just don't use so many crackers that your soup resembles mush.

Stomach growling
Don't draw attention to it. It's a normal bodily function, certainly nothing to be embarrassed about.

SETTING THE TABLE

The first thing your dinner guests will see is the table setting. Make a good impression by paying attention to detail. Whether it's formal or casual, the basics remain the same. Dishware, glassware and flatware should be spotless. Linens should be clean and pressed. Don't worry if you don't have expensive china and sterling flatware. Every item placed on the table should serve a purpose; don't overcrowd your table. Less is better. Place settings should be evenly spaced. Be creative with what you have. Add some brightly colored napkins or an unusual centerpiece, and you'll have an attractive table.

Candles: may be used at any time, but do not burn at eye level.

Centerpiece: must be low enough so that your guests may see one another from across the table.

Coasters: may use them under cold drinks.

Cover: the term for an individual place setting.

Dishes:
Service plate: Not used as much today except in fine restaurants. It is placed in the center of your cover. The first course is set on it. Both service plate and first course plate are removed together. For example if you are served soup, a soup bowl is placed on the service plate. When you are done, set your spoon on the service plate. The waiter will remove your soup bowl, soup spoon and service plate.

Dinner plate:	If the plates have a pattern, set them so the pattern faces the person. Set the plate one inch from the edge of the table. It is used for the main course and accompanying side dishes.
Bread and butter plate:	Set this plate up above the forks. On it we place bread, rolls and butter. Use your butter knife to take the butter.
Salad plate:	Since salad is often a separate course, this plate is set in the center of your place setting. It can be set on the service plate if no prior course has been served. If the main course arrives before you are finished, place the salad plate to the left of the dinner plate and forks.
Cup and saucer:	Are placed to the right of the dinner plate, knives and spoons. Turn the handles to the right so that the right hand may easily pick it up when being used.
Dessert plate:	The best is saved for last and is set in the center. Enjoy!

Flatware

Each place setting may have a dinner knife and fork, salad fork, teaspoon and soup spoon. No more than three of any utensil are set at one time. You may have three forks at your place setting consisting of a salad fork, dinner fork and seafood fork. Later a dessert fork can be brought out with the dessert. Too many forks at one time gets crowded. Line up the silverware from the bottom so the handles are evenly spaced from the table's edge. Flatware is set in the order in which it is used. Start with the outermost utensil first. Once used, all utensils stay on the plates.

Forks:	Are placed on the left side of the plate. Two exclusions to this rule are the dessert fork which can also be set above the dinner plate, and the seafood fork which is set at the right of the spoons. If salad is served before the main course, the salad fork is set to the left of the dinner fork. Some

restaurants serve salad after the main course. In this case the salad fork is placed to the right of the dinner fork. The dinner fork is larger than the salad fork. Begin with the outside fork and work inward.

Knives: Are placed on the right side of the plate. The dinner knife is the largest and is set closest to the plate. Turn the blade inward toward the plate. It is used for cutting food. The smaller butter knife stays on the bread and butter plate with the blade turned in and handle pointing to the right.

Spoons: Set spoons at the right of the knives. Again, set three or less spoons at your setting. The soup spoon is placed on the outer right, and the teaspoon is placed between it and the knives.

Dessert spoon and fork: These may be set with the other flatware. If so, they are placed next to either side of the plate. They also may be placed above the plate with the fork closest to the plate and the handle pointing toward the other forks. The spoon is placed above the fork with the handle pointing toward the other spoons.

Glassware: Glasses are set above the knives and spoons. The water glass is the largest glass. A beverage glass is placed to the right of and slightly in from the water glass. The waiter will pour the correct beverage in the proper glass.

Napkins: I'm still amazed at the number of people who don't even use a napkin. What do they wipe their hands on? Their pants?

Paper napkins are fine for everyday. Cloth napkins are a nice touch and certainly dress up a table. They may be set on the service/dinner plate, laid to the left of the forks or decoratively folded and placed in a glass. A napkin should not be set under the forks. You shouldn't have to pick up your forks to reach your napkin.

Tablecloth: When a cloth is used, please iron it so that it looks fresh and new. Check for spots. It should extend nine to twelve inches below the table on all sides. Buy the correct size cloth for your table.

PLACE SETTING FOR DINNER

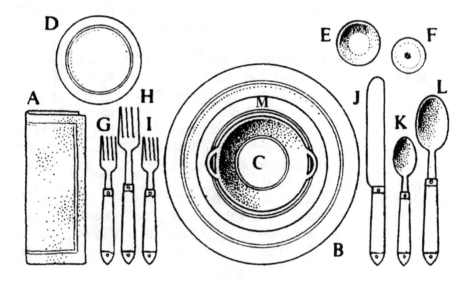

A. Napkin; B. Dinner or service plate; C. First-course bowl; D. Bread and butter plate; E. Water goblet; F. Beverage glass; G. Salad fork; H. Dinner fork; I. Dessert fork; J. Dinner knife; K. Teaspoon; L. Soup spoon; M. Salad plate.

Review

1. You and your family are going to dinner this Saturday at 7:00 p.m. No family members smoke, and it is your mom's birthday. "Phone in" a reservation for this event. Have Mom get on the extension and play the role of the restaurant hostess.

2. When dining in a restaurant, purses and packages should be placed:

3. What may you do if you can't finish your meal?

4. It's impolite to ask the waiter what a certain term on the menu means.   True or False

5. If you eat three meals per day, how many meals do you eat every year?

6. You've just been served an appetizer, and you don't know the proper way to eat it. What should you do?

7. List two times when it is necessary to leave the table.

8. Is it proper to cut up an entire piece of meat at one time?

9. Licking your fingers is acceptable.   True or False

10. How do you know which utensil to use first?

11. You should bite down on your
    fork while eating.   True or False

12. What are fingerbowls used for?

13. Which are fork foods?

deviled eggs   cupcakes

grapes   chicken (in a restaurant)

cookies   french fries

rolls   bacon

14. Napkins are placed _____ while dining.

15. Food is passed to the _____.

16. Describe proper posture at the table.

17. It is acceptable to decline a first serving.   True or False

    You may decline a second serving.   True or False

18. A server should serve you on your _____ side.

19. Dirty plates should be removed from your _____ side.

20. Should people smoke at the table while others are still dining?

Place Settings

21. The term for an individual place setting is: _____.

22. Forks are placed on the _____ side of the plate. Two exceptions are:

23. Glasses are set:

24. Draw a place setting below, using the following pieces:

dinner plate	dessert fork
soup spoon	salad fork
teaspoon	napkin
water glass	dinner knife
beverage glass	salad plate
dinner fork	bread & butter plate
first course bowl	

PERSONAL GROOMING

Personal grooming gives you an attractive appearance and helps develop self-confidence. Develop a daily grooming routine. As you grow older, change it to adapt to your needs. Personal grooming is one way of showing consideration for others. Appearance is very important to your image. There is no substitute for that polished, put-together look.

GROOMING ROUTINE

DAILY

____bathe or shower

____brush teeth 2 - 4 times

____use anti-perspirant

____brush hair often

____exercise

____wash hair (as often as needed)

____cleanse skin twice daily

____clean eyeglasses

____wear freshly-laundered clothing

____shave underarms and legs

____drink eight glasses of water

____apply sunscreen to face and hands

WEEKLY

____manicures

____facial mask

____pedicures

____polish shoes

EIGHT WEEKS

____trim hair, especially bangs

____get a new toothbrush

____deep condition hair

____clean out your closet

SIX MONTHS

____dental checkup

YEARLY

____physical examination

S.O.S SAVE OUR SKIN

The old saying, "Beauty is only skin deep," reminds us of the importance of proper skin care. As your body's largest organ, skin completely covers you, so don't take it for granted.

Our skin works constantly to protect us from the invasion of harmful bacteria entering the body. It regulates your body temperature, keeping it at 98.6 degrees, excretes salts and harmful toxins, cushions internal tissues from minor injuries, and renews itself by forming new cells every 28 days. With all that your skin does for you, shouldn't you pamper and protect it?

DO:
- use a sunscreen, especially on face and hands. Use it all year round, not just in summer.
- cleanse twice a day. Rinse well. Use warm, never hot, water.
- use a toner to help maintain your pH balance.
- moisturize with a product designed for your skin type. Moisturizers are necessary even for oily skin. It absorbs excess oil where needed, yet keeps those dry patches lubricated.
- get plenty of rest. Most of us need at least 8 hours of sleep.
- exercise to increase circulation.
- drink lots of water. Soda does not count.
- eat several servings of fruits and vegetables every day.
- wear gloves when doing housework, dishes, washing the car.

DON'T:
- tan or expose your skin to the sun's UV rays without protection. Avoid any degree of sunburn. The sun you get during childhood and teen years does the most damage. If you use sunscreen now, you won't look 50 when you're only 30. A tan is your skin's response to injury from the sun.
- smoke. It increases wrinkles, ruins the skin and is deadly.
- frown or squint. Wear sunglasses.
- touch your face or lean on your hands.
- go to bed without cleansing your face.
- sleep on your stomach. Sleeping on your back is best.

KNOCKOUT NAILS

Neglect your nails? Never! Not after noticing these nifty notes.

- Your nails are not a finger food. Do not bite them.
- Wear rubber gloves faithfully while doing dishes and cleaning with household chemicals.
- Your nails are not a substitute for screwdrivers, pliers or tweezers.
- Wear gloves when you go outside in cold weather.
- Use a pen to push the buttons on the telephone.
- Carry a nail clipper and emery board with you to quickly trim hangnails and snags.
- Use hand lotion several times a day. Massage the lotion into your cuticles.
- Don't peel off nail polish. You're taking off layers of nail with it.

GIVE YOURSELF A WEEKLY MANICURE

Choose a place to do your nails that is quiet and has plenty of space. The kitchen table is great. Set a towel, placemat or paper towels on the table. You don't want to spill nail polish or remover on the table. Have everything ready. And have fun!

Use a non-drying nail polish remover and either cotton balls or tissues. Put some remover on a tissue and hold on the nail for 5 seconds to help soften the polish so it comes off easier. Remove all polish.

Soak nails a few minutes in warm, soapy water. This removes all traces of nail polish remover, keeps nails from breaking during filing and softens cuticles.

If nails need to be clipped, use clippers and cut straight across. Be careful not to cut too much.

File nails in one direction, not back and forth. Use an emery board.

Shape them by leaving straight sides and an ovaled tip. This gives support to the sides.

Gently push back the cuticles by using an orange stick wrapped in cotton. Cuticle creams and oils are available for this step.

Always apply a base coat before applying polish. This protects the nail and helps the polish adhere.

Apply two coats of polish, allowing plenty of time for each coat to dry. Place your hand on the table to steady it while the other hand applies the polish in three brush strokes. The first stroke goes up the center, the next two on either side.

A top coat of clear polish helps nail color last longer. Coat the underside of nails too.

Give your polish time to dry. It's so upsetting to have wet nails that get smudged because you're in a hurry.

TREAT YOUR FEET TO A PEDICURE

Are your feet beat? Do you hide your feet in socks and shoes all winter? When summer comes, do your feet look neglected? With just a little time and effort, your feet can look great!

Remove nail polish with cotton balls or tissues and non-drying remover.

Soak feet in warm, sudsy water for 10 minutes. Use a nail brush to clean under your toenails. Soaking your feet is great after a long day.

Gently rub a pumice stone over the soles of your feet to remove dead, rough skin. Not too hard, please.

Apply foot lotion. Any hand lotion will do. Massage it into your feet paying attention to your heels.

Carefully push back cuticles using an orange stick wrapped with a piece of cotton. Or you can use your towel. It's not a good idea to cut cuticles.

Unlike fingernails which are shaped into an oval, toenails are cut straight across. This prevents ingrown nails. Don't cut too short.

File your toenails, but again only in one direction. Filing in a back and forth motion causes them to become jagged.

Place cotton or tissue between your toes to separate them. Put on your base coat. Let it dry.

Next apply two coats of color letting each dry.

Finish with a top coat to seal in the color.

Prop your feet and relax, read a book or just meditate for ten minutes.

Don't put on socks or shoes until the polish is dry.

Polish applied to toenails always seems to last longer and look better than that applied to fingernails.

If you have foot problems such as ingrown nails, corns or warts, see your doctor.

Your shoes may rub against your feet and cause all kinds of callouses and bumps. Pads are available to place in your shoe to help stop the problem.

Your feet will thank you if you buy shoes that fit comfortably.

One of the best gifts you can receive is a gift certificate for a manicure/pedicure. It's a real treat. Plus you'll learn the proper techniques. Watch and learn. Don't be afraid to ask questions.

SHOPPING SAVVY

When it comes to shopping, there are two kinds of people. The first could walk into any retail store and come out with the perfect outfit in five minutes. The second person could spend all day with a personal shopper and still not feel she has the right outfit. Shopping is a skill that anyone can learn.

Keep a notepad and pen in your closet. When you think of an item you need, write it down. Take this list along when you shop.

Know what you are shopping for before you go. Set a spending limit. Beware of charge card extravagance.

Take your mom, dad or friend whose opinion you value.

If looking to accessorize or match a jacket or pant, take it along.

Try to shop when the stores are less crowded. Early morning and late evenings are a good time.

After one hour of shopping, take a break and then go back to it. This is not a marathon.

Try on everything before you buy. If you are looking for pants or a dress, take along the proper shoes.

Do not buy something just because it is on sale. It's no bargain if you don't have anything to wear with it. Buy only if the item looks good on you and complements your coloring. Be picky.

Shop for comfort. Beautiful but uncomfortable clothes will hang in your closet. That gorgeous sweater that itches just a little bit in the dressing room will itch a lot more when you wear it all day. The same is true for skirts that ride up, shoes that are just a tad snug and pants that are too tight. You'll probably wear them only once.

To get the most out of your wardrobe, buy garments in a few basic colors that coordinate.

Avoid buying trends as they do not stay in style. Once in a while is okay...and fun!

Cleaning Your Closet

Is your closet full of clothing that you've worn just once or perhaps never worn? Maybe you're saving an outfit for a special occasion. Or you have a neat sweater but no pants to match.

It's a great idea to clean out your closet every year. A couple of good dates to do this are the December holidays and your birthday. Those are times you usually get new clothes.

For every new garment you put in your closet, why not throw out an old one?

Be organized. Divide your clothing into the following categories:

Love it, Loathe it, What is it?

Organize the **Love it** items and put them back in your closet. Jackets, shirts, pants, dresses all should have their own closet area.

Take the **Loathe it** items to a charity if they're in good repair. If not, throw them out. By all means, get rid of them. Don't let them sneak back into your closet.

The **What is it** category can be kept separately in your closet for three months to see if you really need it. A good rule of thumb is if you haven't worn something in the past year, you won't start now. Maybe you could find a perfect pair of pants to wear with that chartreuse sweater on your next shopping expedition. That's great if you do, but if you have no success, then get rid of the **What is it** group for good.

IMAGE MAKERS

Having that altogether look is easy once you know how. Follow these pointers.

CLOTHING
- must be clean and spotless
- iron wrinkled garments
- use a lint brush or roller daily
- keep neckline tags tucked down inside
- coordinate clothing; colors and patterns shouldn't clash
- clothing should be properly fitted for your body
- button buttons and zip zippers
- wear blouses with sleeves at work
- wear a camisole or t-shirt under sheer blouses/shirts
- match color of shoes and hosiery or shoes and hemline

ACCESSORIES
- jewelry should add to your image, not distract from it
- scarves must stay in place; scarf pins help
- carry the best purse you can afford
- purse and shoes should complement each other as well as your outfit
- glasses must be smudge-free
- wipe off your shoes after each wearing
- replace worn down heels
- belts need to match the width of the beltloop

GROOMING
- wear hair in a style that holds throughout the day; keep it out of your face
- retouch your makeup throughout the day, especially after eating
- you may brush your teeth after lunch at a restaurant; be discreet and rinse the sink
- carry a toothbrush and dental floss with you
- keep nails well manicured
- touch up chipped nail polish
- exercise three to four times per week; it boosts your system
- maintain a healthy diet

IMAGE BREAKERS

You work so hard at being your best, but one flaw can ruin it all. Avoid these mistakes.

CLOTHING
- soiled or wrinkled garments
- "pilled" and nubby fabric
- missing buttons and loose threads
- visible panty lines
- colored or polka dotted underwear worn with white shorts or pants; buy flesh colored underwear
- see through blouses
- bra or slip strap slipping off shoulder
- dress slip that shows at the hemline; when wearing a slit skirt, match the slit in the skirt with the slit in the slip
- very tight clothing; if it's too small, don't wear it
- t-shirts with tacky/obscene sayings
- clothes that bare too much skin

ACCESSORIES
- scuffed shoes or worn down heels
- hosiery with runs or lots of snags
- rings on every finger or five necklaces
- earrings that jangle especially on the phone
- scarves that "move" around or come undone
- belts with worn notches
- bulging billfolds

GROOMING
- hair that is stringy, dirty or worn so that it hangs in your face
- fingernails so long you can't button clothes or zip pants
- chipped nail polish
- perfume that is overpowering; many people have allergies
- combing hair and retouching makeup in public
- coughing without covering your mouth
- blowing your nose and then shaking hands
- using a toothpick instead of brushing your teeth
- chewing gum
- smoking anytime, anywhere

WHAT'S WRONG WITH THIS PICTURE?

Do you see yourself in any of these situations?

1. Poor posture while standing and sitting

2. Chewing gum or even worse pulling on it with your fingers

3. Gossiping about someone

4. Brushing hair and putting on lipstick in a restaurant

5. Biting fingernails

6. Talking aloud at the movies

7. Making an improper introduction – not saying your name, wimpy handshake, quiet voice, no eye contact

8. Talking very quietly

9. Talking very loudly

10. Using poor grammar – "Um," "Yeah," "Ain't"

11. Complaining to parents about chores

12. Not opening a door for someone; not holding the door open for the person behind you

13. Cutting in line at the cafeteria, a restaurant, etc.

14. Not helping a person who drops papers, a notebook, etc. at school—just walking by or worse yet, stepping on the papers

15. Ignoring a new student in school. Not introducing yourself or asking her to join your group at lunch

16. Talking negatively about your teachers

17. Not listening when someone is talking with you

18. Interrupting someone during your conversation

19. Breaking a promise: "I promised that I wouldn't tell—but guess what I know!"

20. Asking rude questions about weight, age or money

21. Not offering your seat to an elderly person or someone who obviously needs it more than you do in a doctor's waiting room, on a bus, anywhere people are waiting

22. Calling attention to someone's flaws: a pimple, a spot on their shirt, a bad hair day

23. Not responding to an RSVP

24. Dropping in at a friend's home unannounced

25. Returning a borrowed object in poor condition

26. Telephone rudeness:
    Demanding, "Who is this?" (say, "May I ask who is calling, please?")
    Asking, "Guess who this is?" (tell the person your name)
    Asking, "Is Mary there?" (say, "May I please speak with Mary?")
    Chewing gum or eating while on the phone
    Not delivering a message to a family member

27. Not writing a thank-you note, especially for a check/gift that was sent by mail

28. Picking on someone or being very unfriendly to someone just because he/she is younger than you

29. Deliberately excluding someone from a party or event. "We don't want to invite her."

30. Being a sore loser, insulting the winner, saying the contest was fixed

31. Not congratulating the winner

32. Telling lies

33. Complaining that you're bored while visiting at your friend's home

34. Bragging about your house, your clothes, your life

35. Using a toothpick in public

36. Covering your mouth with your hand when you speak

37. Being jealous of your friend's possessions or good fortune

38. Wearing too much makeup

39. Not thanking someone who holds a door open for you, etc

40. Acting unappreciative of a gift you've just opened – even if you really don't like it

41. Sharing someone's makeup or hairbrush

42. Car travel:
    Arguing
    Kicking the seats
    Complaining
    And the always popular, "Are we there yet?"

43. Not answering when asked a question or just nodding your head

GOOD HABITS

Practice them daily and they'll soon become second nature to you.

Be considerate to all family members at all times

Use good grammar every day

Stick to a nutritious and healthy diet

Check your appearance before heading out the door every morning

Wear clothes, jewelry and hair style that add to your image

Keep clothes ironed and clean

Polish shoes and replace run-down heels

Keep nails, both finger and toe, well manicured

Walk and sit with good posture

Be poised in all situations

Keep a positive attitude and let it show to others

Speak to people when spoken to and smile

Write a thank-you note upon receiving gifts and kindnesses

Shake hands using direct eye contact and a smile

Be responsible and dependable; make lists if necessary

Be on time for appointments; if not possible, then call

Be considerate of others in public and at home

Be patient

Be able to handle constructive criticism and rejection

Be persistent; do not put off things

Stick up for your family and friends—actually everyone

Be cheerful, mature and show an interest in all you do

BAD HABITS

Have any bad habits? No? You might be surprised. You have to be aware of them in order to break them.

Thinking only of yourself

Putting off an apology or writing a thank-you note

Breaking promises

Gossiping

Lying

Chewing gum

Bad posture

Wearing clothes that no longer fit you well

Wearing clothes and jewelry that are tacky or in bad taste

Wearing clothes that are wrinkled or in need of repair

Wearing shoes that are dirty, run-down or cracked

Combing hair or reapplying makeup in public

Using toothpicks

Biting finger or toenails

Cracking your knuckles

Covering your mouth when speaking

Looking down when speaking

Using slang terms at anytime: um, yeah, you know

Using profanity

Being noisy at a movie theatre, library, church

Being loud and obnoxious

Neglecting your skin care routine

Wearing too much makeup

Smoking